# COLIN COWIE

# THE gold STANDARD

## GIVING YOUR CUSTOMERS WHAT THEY DIDN'T KNOW THEY WANTED

HarperCollins
Leadership

An Imprint of HarperCollins

To Gertrude Kleszczewski

For your twenty-five extraordinary years of unwavering
service and being the inspiration for this book.

Published by HarperCollins Leadership, an imprint of HarperCollins Focus LLC.

Any internet addresses, phone numbers, or company or product information printed in this book are offered as a resource and are not intended in any way to be or to imply an endorsement by HarperCollins Leadership, nor does HarperCollins Leadership vouch for the existence, content, or services of these sites, phone numbers, companies, or products beyond the life of this book.

ISBN 978-1-4002-2404-3 (eBook)
ISBN 978-1-4002-2400-5 (HC)

Library of Congress Control Number: 2021938576

Printed in the United States of America
21 22 23 24 25 LSC 10 9 8 7 6 5 4 3 2 1

# Contents

# Letter to the Reader

I arrived in Los Angeles in the mid-eighties from South Africa with little money, a well-cut suit, and a suntan. That my life journey was going to be so exciting or rewarding was something I was yet to discover. Early on I learned how important it was to dream big. Once committed to the mind, almost any idea is possible. Over the course of my career, I've designed fabulous parties and worked with the world's biggest celebrities, royalty, and captains of industry. I've written books and designed tableware, furniture, and giftware. I have appeared on national network morning shows teaching people how to live and entertain with style and elegance. I've racked up fifteen million miles traveling the globe in search of the finest examples of experiences, services, and products for my clients.

Although I have lived the ultimate American Dream, it hasn't always been smooth sailing. I weathered many storms in my personal and business lives and each time came out stronger. I've learned that failure, adversity, and vulnerability are opportunities to learn and create a better version of yourself. And because I have a team of people who rely on me, failure has never been an option. I've always found a way to pivot and find a new path.

Who knew how COVID was going to affect the world? I certainly didn't. On February 22, 2020, I married Danny Peuscovich in South Africa. We didn't know our wedding was going to be the last glamorous bash before the world shut down. We came back to New York to lockdown. In early March, I optimistically told my staff that this would go away as quickly as it came. Soon I realized I was wrong. I always thrived when challenged, but this was a challenge to me on every level.

For many years I had wanted to focus on the hospitality sector of the market. This was my golden opportunity; now I had the time to figure out how to make that ambition a reality. While I remained committed to my event design and production company, I watched all our income for 2020 move to 2021 and 2022. So, I pulled my team together and six weeks later, I launched something new: Thrive Hospitality. Six weeks afterward, I had an office, a new home in Miami, and my first signed contract as creative director for a luxury beach resort.

Like so many others, I learned invaluable lessons last year: In the midst of a devastating worldwide pandemic, what had seemed so important became unimportant, and what was unimportant became super important.

Before the pandemic, we didn't need yet another service or another product; almost every industry was already overcrowded. Many vulnerable businesses closed their doors, while others learned how to run their businesses more efficiently and figured out how to keep expenses down and profits up. I wish I had taken these same measures years ago. As I write this, the world is in the process of being vaccinated against the virus and the time when people can gather safely again is in sight. By creating a culture of proactive customer service now, when society starts to open up, we will all be better set up for success. And that is why I wrote this book.

I know I am blessed and I have learned that talents are gifts that are meant to be shared. The more I share, the bigger my platform to give becomes. I believe in absolute generosity. The more you give, the more you receive and then there's more you have to give. I get tremendous joy and satisfaction from supporting philanthropic platforms that service children around education, art, and mentorship programs.

We all need to express gratitude and humility. Too often we move from one accomplishment to the next without taking time to appreciate our success and those who helped get us there, or what we could have done better, or who we might have thanked as we rushed along.

People ask, "When are we going back?" We are *not* going back. *There is no future in the past. We have all changed!* We have accepted new ways of working remotely and doing things differently. Never look back. Focus on looking forward and that's what will get you and all of us to the other side.

*Colin*

# Preface

*Gertrude*

When I was writing this book, I was thinking about what the preface might be. I've been fortunate to have experienced some of the most amazing hospitality the world has to offer. Where did I experience the best customer service? At first, I thought of five-star resorts and exotic safari camps, then I considered the grand hotels and luxury retail experiences. And then it came to me: the best example of customer service I have ever experienced.

Twenty-five years ago, I had just moved into a large apartment on the Upper East Side of New York City and was in desperate need of an efficient housekeeper. I was introduced to a single mother with five great children, by the name of Gertrude Kleszczewski. We hit it off on day one. One week later, she began working for me and since then I have enjoyed the most extraordinary journey with her. Once she began, it felt as though Gertrude had totally dedicated her life to my well-being, safety, and comfort. She became such an important part of my life that when I got married, Gertrude walked me down the aisle with my two sisters dressed in a custom Naeem Khan dress,.

Not only did I love and adore Gertrude, I respected and appreciated her, not just for what she did for me, but for the spirit in which she did everything. When I moved to Miami in the fall of 2020, it was time for her to retire and sadly, time to say goodbye to her in a working capacity. I have missed her ever since.

Gertrude epitomized proactive service. She always looked for an opportunity to do things better. She demonstrated extraordinary attention to detail and an exemplary work ethic. She showed up early every day and never left till the home was immaculate, whether it was 6:00 p.m., after dinner, or after midnight. It didn't matter whether I had dined alone, or there were four, or twenty-four, for dinner. The kitchen and dining room were left spotless, and the bed was turned down. In the twenty-five years she was my housekeeper, I think Gertrude had ten sick days and today she is almost seventy-five!

Gertrude took 100 percent charge of the running of my home. The fresh flowers she bought at the flower market were always tastefully arranged. The refrigerator and freezer were packed with home-cooked soups and stews for winter nights and impromptu dinners. I collect silver, and every piece was always shined and ready to be used. Every piece of table linen was starched and carefully folded.

I have always entertained at home instead of at restaurants. I could call Gertrude from the Hong Kong airport and discuss a menu with her for dinner for eight that night. When I arrived home at 3:00 p.m., the table would be set, there would be beautifully arranged flowers on the table, the wine would be chilling, and dinner would be in the refrigerator, ready to be reheated. Even if I wasn't entertaining that evening, I knew Gertrude's roast chicken would be waiting for me. Everything was impeccably done and always exceeded my expectations. Her food was incredible. With her innate good taste and a natural sense of style, she added a layer of elegance to everything she touched.

I never once saw Gertrude come to work without being excited for the day ahead. She worked with the same passion in her last week as she did the day she started. Besides the day-to-day chores of keeping house, she always created a project. One day it was polishing silver; the next day it was packing the winter clothes for storage or repotting all the houseplants. I love orchids, and Gertrude knew how to get the best bargains for the best flowers. She would buy orchid plants at Trader Joe's and tell the salesperson that she did not need the terra-cotta pots as she was going to replant them herself. That saved a considerable amount of money over the course of a year. I would come home to find a massive bowl planted with ten or fifteen orchids. If Gertrude had gone to a florist for a similar arrangement, it would have cost hundreds of dollars. Her version cost considerably less, looked equally beautiful, and lasted as long.

Gertrude and I were born three days and several decades apart. Like me, she thrives on order. The Container Store was her fix. It seemed like there were more containers in my home than in the Sixth Avenue store in Manhattan, each one carefully labeled with its contents.

Setting up a new home without Gertrude has made me realize again what a truly extraordinary woman Gertrude is, and how much she has taught me about the gold standard of customer service. I miss her every day. She will remain my friend forever.

Clearly, Gertrude epitomizes the gold standard of customer service!

*Colin Cowie*

# Introduction

*A Simple Boy from Africa*

I grew up in Zambia, in Central Africa, in a small town called Kitwe. I recall there was one movie theater, a hotel where you wouldn't want to stay, and a country club. That was it. However, my childhood was never boring. I attribute that to my family, who loved people and knew how to entertain them—and took full advantage of every opportunity to do so.

South Africans are incredibly hospitable people. When you come into our homes you are immediately made to feel welcome. You're offered something to drink and something to eat. Being a gracious and kind host has nothing to do with impressing people. A lot of people throw money at shiny things to impress their guests. That's the easy way. I've always believed that you entertain people by making them feel welcome and comfortable. Those are the two most important things that can create the ever-important emotional connection between you and your guests. It's how I entertain my friends, and it's the heart and core of what I do in my business—by creating longtime relationships that last.

When you try to impress people, the opposite happens—you intimidate the very people you want to get closer to. People simply want to feel genuinely welcomed. Your event may have bling, but if it has no soul it won't make you and those around you feel good. When we create an event at Colin Cowie Lifestyle, it's always about how we make *you* feel.

I can't remember a time when my family wasn't entertaining guests in our home or being entertained at the homes of friends. My father was in the mining business, and my mother was a stay-at-home-mom. I had an older brother, Gordon, and two sisters, Anne and Janet. When I was six, we moved to South Africa and, while there were a lot more things to do with our time, our way of life didn't change very much. The simple lesson my parents taught us was that life is all about the people we surround ourselves with and how we interact with them.

I believe in reincarnation: I think in past lives I was a king, and in others I was a slave. I know how to be served, but I also know how to serve. It's why I'm good at what I do. I'm a giver and a pleaser by nature. I've always been in a place of service and get tremendous pleasure from serving. As a kid I was always setting the table, lighting candles, and decorating the Christmas tree in July. I moved the furniture around so much, my father told me he was going to paint around the furniture so that I wouldn't rearrange it again.

My parents—my father especially—were very strict. We ate with our parents, and they expected we would behave at the table. By the time I was eight years old, I knew the proper way to set a table—even when there were multiple forks and spoons at a place setting—and how to clear. My father tied two dishtowels together and tied them around my shoulders to keep them pressed against the back of that chair so that I would learn to sit without slouching at the table. When that didn't work, I was made to stand and eat. I very quickly learned that lesson, and to this day, I eat with an upright back. We learned to use a knife and fork in the European style—fork in the left hand and knife in the right, so you didn't have to keep switching hands—and how to cut up our food so our plates didn't look like a war zone. We learned how to eat and drink without making noise. From the time I was twelve I was allowed to have a proper glass of wine at Sunday lunch, which was a formal meal at our house. The table was set with the good china and silver, and the best linen. We always had a traditional English roast and the crispiest potatoes. When we were adults with our own households, my late brother, my sisters, and I all claimed to make those potatoes better than the others. I was taught to smell the wine, taste it, talk about it, appreciate it. When I reached the legal drinking age, it wasn't "forbidden fruit," and I never had the urge to go out and get completely wasted, spring-break style. I can't say that's worked for me in later life!

We had to make our beds and keep our rooms tidy and stand when a lady or someone older entered the room. Today I'm often the only man who stands up when a woman walks in; it's ingrained in me, a natural instinct. We had to look people in the eye, shake hands, and introduce ourselves confidently. I was taught how to pour a drink and open a bottle of wine, even though I was too young to partake. My mother used to smoke cigarettes in a fancy cigarette holder in her earlier years; by the time she put the cigarette in the holder, I had to have the lighter out. I resented that discipline when I was a child, but I'm so grateful for it today because wherever I am in the world, I can put my best foot forward. It's one way I stand out as knowing how to be.

Our punishments were taking on house chores. We were put on bicycle cleaning duty for a week, or cleaning school shoes until we saw our faces in the shine, or mending torn clothing or holey socks, or assisting Jerry, our houseman. Looking back now, I understand how valuable those lessons were. My late brother, my sisters, and I all learned to cook, run homes, and entertain fabulously, with confidence and style.

•

## Basic Training For Life

I was a Boy Scout for ten years and picked up many other skills there that have become extremely handy along the way. At school we had summer uniforms, winter uniforms, military uniforms, and sports uniforms. Your hair had to be two fingers above your collar. We were required to wear a hat in summer and carry a small suitcase, not a backpack.

I finished school and was drafted into the South African army when I was sixteen. I turned seventeen on the train to basic training, and by the time I was seventeen-and-a-half I had a high-powered rifle in my hand and was being prepared for operational service. Serving in the South African army was no walk in the park; our training was based on the Israeli military training program. It was very strict, very disciplined. You never dropped your rifle; it was your life and your most trusted possession. Basic training was designed to break you down. You would spend four days preparing for inspection; everything had to be perfect.

I can clearly remember the time when, at 4:00 a.m. the day we were supposed to go on leave after three months of grueling basic training, they woke us up and had us put on the boots we had spent hours cleaning to go running in the mud.

When we came back, they announced that inspection was in two hours. It was impossible to get our kit ready in time, and of course we all failed inspection, which meant leave was canceled. I was utterly demoralized.

After basic training, I was sent to the most remote part of the country to work with armored cars in the Special Service Battalion. This meant I was either going to be a mechanic, a gunner, or a driver. Clearly I was not designed for any of those roles. I needed a plan, an exit strategy. One afternoon, I was one of 3,500 troops on the parade ground with our rifles. Everyone was standing at attention. On cue, I fell to the ground, dropped my rifle, and threw a faked epileptic seizure that Meryl Streep would have been proud of. I got sent to the sick bay and once there I made friends with the captain who was running the operation. She got me transferred to sick bay permanently. Mission accomplished!

## It Started with a Bar in a Tent

As a medic, I got sent to the operational area Oshakati in Namibia, just south of the Angola border and Ondangwa.

I was nineteen and in charge of the sick bay with a doctor and two people to assist me. I ran it *meticulously*. Everything was immaculate and organized. The nearest civilian hospital was forty miles away, so we took care of every imaginable situation, from emergency casualty evacuations, to local women giving birth, to frontline medical injuries. And yes, I know how to deliver a baby. I helped deliver many, though I haven't had to do so since I moved to the United States.

One of my responsibilities was to inspect the kitchen for cleanliness. I made friends with the kitchen crew, and they'd give me big T-bone steaks for the barbecues and parties I'd throw behind the sick bay. Because I was head of the sick bay, I could arrange for you to get sick leave. If your sister was getting married or if . . . I was the person you came to if you wanted to go back home to South Africa for the weekend. Hence, I was very popular.

I became friendly with the commanding officer, a major who was formerly from the Zimbabwean army. My mother would send me care packages, and one in particular contained two very good bottles of Cape wine, a Cabernet Sauvignon. After the wine was confiscated, I reminded the major that it was probably in his office. I offered to share it with him (very cheeky of me to speak to a superior officer that way), and over a glass or two suggested that it would be good for troop morale if I could set up an officer's bar. As soon as he said yes, I requisitioned a tent, a blender, a cassette player with speakers, and other things I needed to set up shop. I wallpapered the tent with rolls of jute and used charcoal to draw sunsets on the walls. I made a fountain from spare parts and put it out front. I called it the Sunset Bar. Every day I served drinks and snacks. I bought a beverage server with a spigot to serve the cocktail of the day. (It was the inspiration for the beverage servers I eventually sold — 150,000 of them! — on Home Shopping Network.) The club was a huge success, and we created one for the enlisted men as well. I created an emotional connection with everyone who walked into the tent. They were entertained and felt at home; they became my friends versus having the experience feel like a transaction. That really was the start of my professional career in hospitality

•

## Entering the Real World

I left the army. When I was twenty-one, I ran a private health spa and conference center on a beautiful estate on 250 acres outside of Johannesburg. We would put on incredible events for Christmas parties and corporate training retreats. Sometimes there would be four events going on at once, with hundreds of guests at a time. We were very, very busy. Being on the outskirts of Johannesburg on a working farm came with its challenges, like intermittent power failures. I was always anticipating someone's arrival, making sure that their room was as welcoming as possible: music was playing, the lights were on, the drapes drawn, and ice was in the ice bucket. I did anything and everything—filled in for the waitstaff, jumped behind the bar, replenished buffets, worked the phones, paid the staff. I even worked the earthmovers one day after a heavy rain when the road was partially washed away and we had guests arriving later that day.

I also learned the hard way that sometimes I had to pay the staff on alternate Fridays, because after they got paid they'd all get drunk and call in sick the next day. I got tired of the one-man show. This way at least half of the team would show up for work.

•

## Out of Africa

I had grown up in racially charged South Africa, and by the time I was twenty-three, I could no longer live with the injustice of apartheid. I couldn't see a future for myself there. I decided if I was going to make a move, now would be the time to do it. In 1985 I got myself a tourist visa and got on a plane to Los Angeles. I had a well-cut suit, a suntan, an exotic accent, big dreams, and $400 in my pocket. After living under strict apartheid in South Africa, I was blown away by LA. I took to it like a duck to water. It did not take me long to get settled and organized. Before I bought a car, I hired a live-in housekeeper who knew how to iron sheets and cook. I had my priorities.

I knew that I wanted to do something in the entertainment industry, and I quickly realized I was more interested in people than performing. While I didn't know exactly what I wanted to do, I decided to leverage my experiences in the army by running the spa/conference center to get a start in the hospitality business.

I started working for a small catering company, Jeanson's. I worked as a waiter. I worked in the kitchen. I worked as a bartender. After three months, I knew the rental companies who supplied the table settings, tents, and furnishings. I knew the best florists. I knew where to get the waiters. I knew how to cook (of course). With that knowledge and my growing contacts, I knew I was going to make it in LA.

I started from scratch and built my business from the ground up. I began doing small parties on my own for eight to sixteen people. I'd get up super early and go to the flower market, the grocer, and the fish market myself. I would design the party and the table settings. I would cook, wait on tables, and clean up after the party. I called my company Colin Cowie Lifestyle, and one small party led to another, usually bigger, party. I was fortunate to find people who were willing to take a chance on a young entrepreneur and who wanted to work with me to set a new standard in hospitality—or as I still like to call it, hospitainment.

I had been invited to a luncheon at the home of Larry and Laurie Turman. He was the producer of *The Graduate*. Mrs.

Turman told me they were hosting a luncheon at their home in Malibu for the Museum of Contemporary Art for Count Panza, who was donating his art collection to the museum. I catered the lunch with a cooking partner, Adriana Pacifici, a wonderful woman who came from Rome. She became a very dear friend and partner, and her connections also helped me find clients.

We landed a job with Jerry Perenchio, one of the legendary producers in Los Angeles. Through him I met Sherry Rivera, Geraldo Rivera's ex-wife. She was dating this young guy named Bruce Willis. She'd met him at a bar on the Upper West Side, and he'd come to LA to be in a show called *Moonlighting*. I did his very first party. I took inspiration from the magic of LA: it was held on Carbon Beach in Malibu. We made a huge bonfire on the beach and I hired the hottest waiters — strong, beautiful guys and gorgeous, sexy girls — and dressed them in white shorts and white tank tops. It was packed with celebrities. Stallone was there, and so was Barbra Streisand. Bruce was very happy, and although it was my first party for him, it was not the last time we worked together. He appreciated my refreshing and collaborative approach, and my commitment to creating a stellar experience for his guests. I did countless parties for him. He married Demi Moore and I ended up doing the interior design for his nightclub, the Mint, and movie theater in Sun Valley, Idaho.

## Creating a New Standard

Before I came to the US, planning parties and events was the job of the wife or the social secretary. She (almost always she) handled the invitations, the seating, arranged for the flowers, and dealt with the caterer, the band, and rental companies. You couldn't rent a club or other interesting venue. There was one style of invitation. In those days, when you rented linens, they were polyester. You got white folding chairs. There were three kinds of china, all white: plain and inexpensive or with a silver or gold rim. There wasn't anyone building props or designing the setting or scripting and orchestrating the guests' experience.

I was an innovator. I changed the playing field. I added drama and production values to events that had followed the same—let's be honest—boring template. I created an *experience in the moment that would create lasting memories.* I would design an event from the ground up so that everything worked together. The color of the invitation reflected the color of the flowers and décor. I would custom design linen tablecloths, place mats, and napkins. I used overlays with fringes and tassels and did things no one else was doing at the time.

I learned how to scale food service. It's one thing to make lamb chops for four, another to make them for forty, and another to make them for four hundred. I've since done events for over two thousand people where I've built ten separate kitchens staffed by ten culinary teams, to serve 250 guests per kitchen and ensure each person got their food properly cooked and served in a timely way. More recently, I did an event in Qatar for two thousand guests and had to figure out how to cook and serve a baby camel, which is a delicacy there, to every four tables from a Guéridon (a fancy silver trolley on wheels). *That* was a challenge.

When I started out, dishes were labor intensive and elaborate. I served caviar twenty different ways. I traveled all over the world and brought back ideas that found their way to the clients' tables: caviar on scrambled eggs in an eggshell; beggar's purses, which were paper-thin crepes filled with caviar and tied with chives; handmade ravioli filled with chicken liver mousse. I was inspired by the French masters, and nouvelle cuisine caught my eye. I planned trips and visited as many of their restaurants as possible, buying their cookbooks and finding ways to bring new ideas home. Times have changed and so has my taste. Now I take a much simpler approach: I seek out the world's finest ingredients and do as little to them as possible.

If I was using outside creative partners (the term I prefer instead of *vendors*), I made sure everyone was working in the same direction to keep the energy going. I established protocols for everyone I worked with—musicians, caterers, photographers, florists—and our contracts reflected that. I put down exactly what was expected: when people would arrive, when they would leave, how they would be dressed, how and where they would be fed, overtime costs. For example, I wanted non-stop music, so I had the band stagger the musicians' breaks, or made sure there was canned music to fill in while they were offstage. I started doing presentations of the event design and table settings, and tastings for the clients so they would know what they were spending their money on. Each time, the events got more elaborate and twice as fabulous.

I was doing very, very unusual things that people had never seen before: covering a pool with a glass dance floor, adding different-colored carpets, and draping thousands of yards of silk across the ceilings of tents. I made massive topiaries out of sugar-crusted fruit for dessert buffets. I brought in people to custom roll cigars for the guests. No one was doing anything like that. I was in a whole different realm and a whole different league.

I'm still known for my meticulous attention to detail and sense of drama. I love to use light and darkness to create magical moments. At one wedding, the bride wore a dramatic black vintage wedding dress. The altar was filled with candlelight and ponds of floating candles. I worked with my lighting director to create an epic bridal walk down the aisle: a pool of light followed the bride's every step as she approached her soon-to-be husband. It was breathtaking!

For a celebrity birthday party, we built a glass table inside a wine cave, as well as a full working kitchen. Each guest had a dedicated server. When the guests were seated, all fifty servers entered the cave at the same time and put each guest's first course down in perfect unison. They repeated the performance for each of the remaining seven courses. The dinner was one of the most memorable culinary experiences that anyone had ever been a part of and exceeded my client's high expectations. It required hours and hours of rehearsals over three days—and the final effect was worth it!

Because I've always been a very, very curious person, when I traveled I would explore different cultures and come home with a myriad of new ideas, fabrics, or unique serving styles. When I was living in Los Angeles, I loved visiting the food halls at Harrod's in London and Macy's Marketplace and bringing back what I learned and tasted.

Every event was different because every client is different. Their event reflected *their* tastes, desires, and personalities. It was unique. It was personal. If it was a Mexican dinner, I used a red-hot chili pepper as a place card, and I wrote the guest's name in gold pen. In Los Angeles I took advantage of all the prop and costume houses, the backdrop houses, and everything else the movie industry had to offer. I felt like an artist who had been painting with his feet in black and white and had discovered Technicolor and a paintbrush he could use with both hands.

My first big wedding was for Ted Field, the heir to the Marshall Field's fortune. I designed the most exquisite tents, with the interiors draped lavishly in miles of white fabric. The tables were covered in satin underlays with draped brocade and fringed overlays. It was very, very fancy. Because this was Hollywood and I had access to movie industry resources, I went to a costume house and rented white military uniforms with gold buttons for the waiters. I decorated the tables with thirty thousand white roses, which was a sizable number in those days. (I've since used a million flowers at one event.)

The wedding that really brought me into the public eye was Hugh Hefner's wedding to his second wife, Kimberley Conrad, in 1989. It was a black tie event at the Playboy Mansion, and they wanted to do a buffet in the garden. I literally built an extension of the house. Black tie and buffets don't usually go hand in hand, so I had to be creative. There's nothing elegant about standing in line for your food in a tuxedo or evening gown and high heels. I divided the menu into four courses served from four identical buffets, which today I would refer to as food stations. We began with a caviar course followed by grilled meats and vegetables, then an extravagant cheese course and finally a magnificent Viennese dessert table. The buffet tables were fronted by waterfall drapes. Announced by trumpeters, the drapes lifted to reveal each course then closed when the guests were finished so the tables could be reset. The decoration of the buffets and the waiters' outfits changed with each course, adding a big dose of glamour, which made for a fitting and appropriate presentation for a black tie dinner.

I took Hollywood by storm. People started to become aware of what it meant and felt like to go to a Colin Cowie event. The events and parties started getting bigger and bigger and more and more elaborate and glamorous. We did Moroccan parties, country western parties, seventies disco and Bollywood-themed parties. Anyone who wanted something fun, crazy, chic, and different came to me. I was the number-one party planner there. I could no longer take on all the work that I wanted and had to get a proper office with staff, assistants, and producers.

Now totally in my stride, I got a call from a startup magazine, *InStyle*. Would I like to be a contributing editor? And by the way, could I introduce them to my celebrity clients? I did entertaining articles for them, and my clients, like Demi Moore, would appear on the cover. I did their Oscar party and Elton John's AIDS Foundation Oscar parties. A producer from *The Oprah Winfrey Show* attended one of the parties; she called and asked me to come on her show.

•

## The Oprah Effect

I have such tremendous respect for Oprah, and I had no idea what effect she would have on my brand. Appearing on her show literally made me a household name. I could be walking through the airport in Madrid, Cape Town, or Hong Kong and people would recognize me. She showcased my work, including a one-hour special that was dedicated to how I create over-the-top events, and one on fantasy weddings. She gave me the opportunity to work with her at some of the most extraordinary historic events like the Civil Rights Legends Ball, and the Legends Who Paved the Way Tribute in 2014, which honored twenty-five African American women in art, entertainment, and civil rights. I don't think I've ever been surrounded by such greatness as I was at these events.

I was honored to produce Oprah's fiftieth birthday at the Bel-Air Hotel and later that night a very grand affair in Montecito where Stevie Wonder performed. There was Sidney Poitier's seventy-ninth birthday celebration at Quincy Jones's home. We called it "To Sidney with Love," and Lulu, who sang the title song for the movie *To Sir, with Love*, sang the song at the party. We did gospel brunches at Oprah's home in Montecito, book parties, Oscar parties, and a party in Chicago celebrating the end of her iconic television show. She paid me the ultimate compliment when she told me, "I don't trust many people, but I trust you implicitly."

And here's a fun fact: I taught Oprah to drink tequila. She came to the opening of the One & Only Palmilla in Cabo San Lucas; it was also John Travolta's fiftieth birthday. As you arrived at the party, you got a shot of tequila. Later, she was making scrambled eggs in the Palmilla kitchen with Quincy Jones at sunrise. There I was, drinking Don Julio 1942 in Quincy Jones's kitchen with Quincy, Oprah, and Gayle King. Not bad for a simple boy from Africa.

The only downside—if you want to call it a downside—of all that exposure was that people thought that only people who were as wealthy as Oprah, heads of state, and royalty could afford to work with me. Of course, that's not true; my company's services aren't *in*expensive, but they are in line with other top-tier event planners. That said, I wouldn't change a thing: Oprah is one of the reasons people think of me as the premiere event and party planner, and for that I will be extremely grateful until my last breath.

●

## The Next Exciting Chapter

In 1996 my first book, *Effortless Elegance with Colin Cowie*, was published. There was an all-star book party at Bergdorf Goodman. I traveled to Chicago and launched the book on *The Oprah Winfrey Show*, then toured the country appearing on morning television shows and doing tabletop appearances at Macy's, Nordstrom, and Bloomingdale's. Lenox approached me to design an eponymous line of china, crystal, silver, and linens.

I was tired of Hollywood and celebrities who thought I should work for them for free. My ever-curious nature needed new challenges. So, I thought, "Maybe it's time I should go to New York."

So, in 1997, I did. I thought that I'd be there for a couple of months, maybe a year. I rented my apartment in Los Angeles to Ellen DeGeneres, who was just getting started. How funny is that? I never returned to Los Angeles to live, though I keep offices there to this day.

When I got to New York, I started to get even bigger projects. People who had seen the fabulous parties I was doing for Oprah called. I started doing corporate work. I orchestrated the opening of the Atlantis Royal Towers in the Bahamas. I was being hired for projects in the Middle East and was now traveling to Qatar, Dubai, and Saudi Arabia. My clients would spend $20 to $25 million for the most lavish royal weddings and events, but no matter how big or small the project was, my goal was always the same: produce flawlessly, exceed expectations, and make people's dreams come true.

I've never been a sycophant, a *yes* person. I always want to make my client look good and present the best version of themselves. One client didn't want to do assigned seating; she just wanted to let people find a table. She was worried that someone wouldn't like their seat. I said, "Susan, out of a hundred guests, two people will be upset with you but ninety-eight will love you for balancing the energy at the table and for taking the time to do a well-thought-out seating plan." I was right, and she was the first person to find me after the party and tell me so.

•

## You Can't Keep a Busy Man Down

I had my pick of the best projects, and I never, ever thought it was going to change. Even after the market crash at the end of the 1980s and after 9/11, business always bounced back. But, when the financial crisis hit in 2008, the world was fundamentally changed and business came back very differently. Advertising changed. Budgets that were spent between newspapers, TV, and magazines were now being shared between internet sites, banner ads, and bloggers. The internet was wild and disruptive. Instead of exclusive relationships with creative partners — florists, musicians, caterers — everyone had their own website, and anyone could contact them with a click. With everyone having access, the world became democratized and you could buy goods directly.

The event business became an unregulated business with no barrier to entry. I woke up one morning and instead of four or five competitors there were ten thousand event and wedding planners with almost no experience who charged half the amount I did. Today, I'm competing not just with my peers in the top tier of the hospitality business; I'm competing with Suzy Smith down the road whose office is her laptop on the dining room table. She's got a pretty website with beautiful pictures that she screen-clipped from other sites, sometimes from mine! I've never seen the world more competitive or more flooded with products and services than what we have today with people so eager to have a job that they are giving away product. I knew I couldn't compete on price. I had to find a better way to differentiate myself from the rest of the pack. Now more than ever, it's important to set yourself apart from the culture of churn and burn.

I never went to university to learn how to run a business. I'm self-taught and learned through trial and error. Whether I've had one employee or fifty-five, I've tried to create a company culture that demands excellence from myself and everyone who works with me. I would have done the same whether I was the CEO of an insurance company or the owner of a gas station. The lessons I've learned can be scaled to any size company, and adapted to any business, even if someone works alone at their kitchen counter. I happen to be in the service business, but don't we all have a customer to serve?

I've always liked being ahead of the curve. The challenge for me is to keep my focus on the present while planning for the future. My event company is often working on five or six projects over the course of a year, all in different stages of production. I'm consulting in the hospitality space for hotels, country clubs, and real estate developers. Even though the COVID-19 pandemic dramatically changed the event business, people will always have occasions to celebrate. Once again, I faced a downturn in business, and once I again I've had to change how I work to fit a new world.

The skills I learned as a kid and the challenges I faced as a young soldier, trying to bring a little light into a dark situation, have stayed with me throughout my career. They inform how I approach each and every project I take on. The attention to detail and unrelenting focus on creating an experience that will stay with my clients for years to come will always win out over price point. No matter how big or small the project, my goal is always the same: to make my client happy and to exceed their expectations by creating special moments and indelible memories.

THE

gold

STANDARD

# one

*Grabbing Attention*

*in a Saturated Market*

I n today's world consumers are overwhelmed with choices in every aspect of their lives. We live in a buyer's world. It's up to you to identify and meet their needs, not the other way around. There's not one nail salon in town; there are fifteen. There aren't two food delivery services; there are ten. In New York City, the price of a Yellow Cab medallion, which used to cost over a million dollars, now costs between $120,000 and $150,000. Why? Competition from disrupters like Lyft and Uber who make the customer experience a priority. Your customer has choices, and you still want the product or service they buy to come from you.

Not only do you have a choice of hair salons, appliances, jeans, you name it, you have choices about *how* you access what you want. I can get my favorite brand of jeans from their own brick-and-mortar store, Nordstrom, Amazon, and two other shopping websites. If you go online to look for a hotel, you have nine competing websites—and that's not including the hotel's own website—offering the same rooms, often at a deep discount.

If you're like me, you don't have the time, the energy, or the interest to go through every option for every choice of product or service you have to make. So how do you make sure your target customer picks you? How do you get—and keep—your potential customers' attention?

A. **You have to have the right product.** Talking about Apple products, Steve Jobs said that you have to start with the customer experience and work backward to the technology. If you don't have what the customer wants, all the marketing in the world won't get them to buy it.

B. **You have to package it fabulously.** Fabulous doesn't mean baroque and gilded. Look at the design esthetic of Apple, Tesla, and Sonos.

C. **You have to make the customer's experience a priority.**

## Know Your Market

This is where in-depth market research, and even some competitive "secret shopping," comes in. Who else is providing the same service or product? How is it different from yours? Is it more innovative? Does it have more features? What about their website? Their pricing? What are their delivery and return policies? How do they deal with refunds? Once you know that, how can you beat them on every single point? Find out exactly what your competition is charging. What are they giving away? What incentives are they offering? You don't have to hire an expensive consulting firm; place an order or make an appointment where you can. What was the experience like? Use the product. Use the service. How is yours better? If it's not better, how is it different? Can you identify a different segment of the audience and find a way to reach them?

Let's look at skincare. Walk into a Sephora store, or even a drugstore, and you'll see how a simple product like moisturizer can be tweaked and positioned to appeal to users with different skin issues (oily, dry, aging, sensitive), demographics (teens, adults, "mature"), and markets (inexpensive with simple plastic packaging to super–high end products encased in elegantly designed containers). How about men's clothing? A button-down shirt is a button-down shirt, right? Not once the founder of UNTUCKit got tired of looking sloppy when he wore his shirt outside his pants and reworked the proportions of the traditional button-down shirt so it looked good untucked.

At Colin Cowie Lifestyle, we recognized we were leaving a lot of business on the table because of the perception that all we handled were clients that had a million dollars or more to spend on an event. We knew that there were customers out there who had amazing events and parties to throw, but they had written us off based on the perception that we only served the uber rich and the uber famous. As a result, we were losing out on great opportunities and the revenue that came with them.

To counter the perception around our price point, we created a new brand architecture by defining three different company divisions, each selling a specific version of the Colin

Cowie experience. At the top end, there is Colin Cowie White. These are the most expensive events, the haute couture experience. If you can afford it, the word *no* does not exist and each element of the event is unique, larger, better, and more fabulous.

The next tier is Signature Colin. I'm on the phone calls, I sit in on the client meetings, and I hold your hand every inch of the way together, working with a designated team.

Finally, there's Team Cowie, which is our fastest-growing division and provides our gold standard of service at a lower price point. While I approve the creative aspects of the event, the client works with team members who I have educated and worked with over the years.

This is a classic example of looking at the market, seeing what our competitors are doing, looking at what we're losing, and putting all of that information to use to increase our market share.

The number of choices available to consumers has grown far more rapidly than the number of consumers. If you can't get your potential customers' attention, you have to accept a smaller piece of the pie in a crowded market where your competitors are undercutting prices, beating you on the product, service, or the experience they are offering. The most effective way to differentiate yourself from the competition and win business is by giving focused attention to the non-tangibles — your client/staff relationships — what I call *the gold standard*: exceptional customer service.

I take a 360 degree approach to attracting attention. Ask yourself: Where do my business and what I'm offering fit into the bigger picture of my industry? Look at every touch point where your team and you engage with your potential client. The equation for the gold standard of service isn't $1 + 1 = 2$. It's $1 + 1 = 3$. What can you do or offer that will keep you ahead of the curve? What can you do to make your product and customer service better than anyone else's? I ask myself those questions every day. I have learned over the years to make sure that my team has dotted every *i* and crossed every *t* before going to an event site. I take pride in assuring my client that we have planned out every detail, ensuring a smooth installation and event as well as being able to handle any unforeseen issues. Knowing this, my clients are able to relax and enjoy their event.

## Be Visible

Before you can get their attention, your customer needs to be able to find you. In today's market that starts with a website. People are very visually driven. Your customer's first encounter with your company is probably through a web search and your website. I know if someone tells me about an interesting product, my first question is "What's the website?"

You may have the best website and the best product, but if you don't have the right SEO (search engine optimization) or aren't using longtail keywords you're not going to come up on the first search page and your customer may not be able to, or have the patience to, find you. Are you active on the right social media for your target audience, and placing your online ads on the right sites? Are you using hashtags to extend your reach beyond your network? These traffic drivers are constantly changing, and staying on top of the changes is important to maintaining the connection to your customers and mining for new ones.

I know I'm impatient; I review the first five links of my top ten search results, and invariably one of those five is who I end up doing business with—if they can provide me what I'm looking for. It's why you used to see companies like AAA Plumbing in the Yellow Pages. Keep your URL short and simple; there's far less chance that someone will type it incorrectly.

Your website is your virtual business card. What does your landing page tell your customer? What's their first impression? You want the page to be attractive and up-to-date in terms of design, but this is one place where flashing lights and moving parts aren't always a good thing. The old naval design principle stands the test of time: KISS, or Keep It Simple, Stupid. Timing is very important: your customer wants the information and images to load quickly, whether they've gone directly to the site or they're clicking on a link. If they're using their cell phone, your mobile application should be readable and easily navigated in the smaller format and should be able to load when your customer doesn't have full cell service.

Invest as much in your back-end as your front-end software. Your landing page may be beautiful, but if your customer can't find what they're looking for, and *fast,* they're going somewhere else. If they have problems with your payment page, they will leave. If your customer is having issues with payments, or returns, this is not the time for a canned response. That's not the story you want customers to tell, and not the way you want to stand out.

Your website or point of sale is a portal not just for your customer to get information about you, but an opportunity for you get information about your customer by offering an opt-in to periodic emails or a newsletter. What you do with that information can determine how they feel and what they say about you. Understanding your customer begins with a courtship: being able to read between the lines and figure out how you customize your connection so that it becomes a long-standing relationship. When is it too much, and when is it too little? What format do they want, what information do they want to see, when and how do they want to receive it? How do you determine what the right amount of engagement is? I have this with a couple of blogs and newspapers that I subscribe to. I can get the information once a week, every morning, or in the evening. I can decide what topics I'm interested in and rank them in the order in which I want to read them. It's my choice. A big part of providing this kind of customized service is knowing who your audience is and what they're looking for. You can let your customer decide! Are they looking for frequency or the most recent information? Do they want to hear from you once a week or only when you have something new or important to tell them, like the announcement of a new product or a sale?

You can't get people's attention if they don't know who you are and why they should want your product or service. Getting noticed means putting what you have to offer in front of the public. Every time my company gets an accolade, or someone mentions us in print, on the air, or on the web, we send links to our clients and friends. They often share the links with their friends or post it on their social media. Sometimes two or three other articles have been written about me and the company because someone saw the first one.

No matter how stellar your product or website, how precise your SEO, or how much money you put into advertising or marketing, the most powerful tool you have is word-of-mouth. That's why companies have spent so much time and money courting internet influencers, and more recently experts and specialists. The time of the influencer is waning; as consumers become more discriminating and discerning, they want information from someone at the top of their field who knows what they're talking about or from someone who has already used your product.

Your customers' stories—good and bad—are what others listen to. When your customers praise or criticize your service, that's what others believe. I was working with a client and we went to London to look for venues. One space I wanted to look at was the one she wouldn't consider because a friend of hers had attended an event there and didn't like it. She conflated the space (which was perfect for her party) with her friend's experience of the event (she didn't like the food, the décor, or the entertainment), and couldn't see beyond that. I came to the space without that bias and only saw what a perfect fit it would be for my client's event. I was finally able to persuade her to use it, but it took a lot of time and talking to get her to see my point of view. It goes to show you how powerful the voice of a credible source is.

On the positive side, a friend's husband had his teeth whitened at his dentist's office. When he asked how he could maintain them, she told him he didn't need to use anything fancy; Colgate Optic White toothpaste and mouthwash would do it. Of all the many, many options available, that's what he continues to use.

Devacurl, a product line for curly hair, is a more cautionary tale. The products were touted and promoted by influencers and beloved by a strong community until stories of scalp irritation, hair loss, and damaged hair began to emerge. Complaints became so vociferous and widespread that the company now faces a class-action lawsuit. The voices of the same influencers and consumers who helped make the brand a success dramatically reduced the company's sales—and even more important, tarnished their reputation. That's not the kind of attention you want.

●

## What's *Your* Customer Looking For?

The gold standard of customer service is not just about how engaging you and your product are; it's about how you engage *with* your customer. The key touch points of engagement are much the same for every business. Your website, of course. Your physical space if you have one: a brick-and-mortar outlet or office. Your employees, whether they're customer facing or not. The experience your customer has with your product or service—how much it satisfies their needs or brings added value to their experience. The delivery of your product or service, and how you deal with any issues that arise. The easier, more efficient, and more pleasurable you can make your customer's experience, the more likely they are to return, and the more likely they are to recommend you to others and become *your* storytellers. There was a time when I wouldn't use Amazon myself; I'm not the most gifted when it comes to technology, and I found ordering complicated. My assistant handled those purchases. Then Amazon implemented one-click ordering, and I've never looked back.

A friend goes to a little coffee shop in her town that's right across the street from a Starbucks. She's fussy about her tea order and has an unusual name that many people don't pronounce correctly and few spell correctly. The first time she went, she gave her order and the barista asked for her name. She said, "I'll give you my Starbucks name." It was simpler to pronounce and almost impossible to misspell. The barista's response? "Give me your real name and tell me how to spell it correctly. We'll get it right." They did, and every time she goes back they greet her by name, and her name is spelled correctly on her cup. Is the coffee at the local shop better than Starbucks? That's a question for debate. Is the experience better? Definitely.

·

## Comparing Apples and Oranges: Service vs. Product

There's a difference between delivering customer service when you're selling a product and when you're delivering a service. You can put ten different products—coffee makers, shampoos, sweaters—in a line and they speak for themselves. Customer service revolves on how easy it is to find and buy those products, and what kind of extras—a longer warranty, free shipping, no-questions-asked returns, a seamless user experience with your website—you give your customer. Every minute a customer has to wait for a service representative to troubleshoot their defective product increases the risk that you've lost them as a customer. It also increases the risk that they won't have anything good to say about your company or your product.

Comparing ten similar services is harder because you have to *experience* service. As a provider, being as proactive as possible and putting the right choices in front of your customer is essential. Going out on a limb and telling your customer, "This is what we're giving you because we think you'll like it," may feel a little scary, but that's what's needed. How do you make your customer feel not just welcome, but cared for? You meet their needs, immediately. You meet the needs they didn't even know they had. Many websites, for example, have a "You may also like" feature, suggesting similar or complementary products. Many fashion websites will style an item multiple ways, showing how a pair of pants can be dressed up or down with shoes, a top, and jewelry, which are all available on the website, of course. At Colin Cowie Lifestyle, we curate the choices we present to our clients based upon our knowledge of the best services in the industry. For example, based on our client's needs, we can suggest the three best photographers who will align with their tastes within their price point.

I was staying at The Boca Raton in Florida on an extended business trip. I'd been there four days and exhausted all the on-site options for dinner. At lunch on the fifth day, I asked the young waitress who was taking care of us if there were any other places to eat in the area. She told me she'd come up with some suggestions, and when she gave me the check, she also handed me a handwritten note with the names, addresses, and phone numbers of four restaurants. "I just spoke with my friends behind the bar," she told me, "and these three restaurants are within a fifteen-minute drive. This one is thirty-five minutes away, but it's worth the trip." She went on to tell me about why she thought I'd have a wonderful experience there. I had only asked for other options, but she took it upon herself to find me more than I expected and went above and beyond. That got my attention. I was asking for a reference to a competitor and they didn't think twice about the request; their concern was for *me*. As a result, I was back at the hotel restaurant the next day.

In the middle of the pandemic, hotels were doing their best to make their guests feel safe and secure. This involved stripping some of the amenities that make staying away from home so pleasurable. I was traveling on business and wanted to order room service. For sanitary reasons, there were none of the usual guides to hotel services or menus. I called room service, was given my menu options, and ordered dinner and a bottle of wine for me and my companion. Let's just say it was an expensive meal. When the food arrived, I was handed a brown paper bag filled with polystyrene containers and disposable utensils. Was the food delicious? Yes. But it was as expensive as it would have been if served on a trolley with a tablecloth, glassware, china, and silverware.

Imagine what it's like to be on the receiving end of your service or product. Creating and living that scenario in your head can change your perspective. If you take something away, you have to give something back. It's only right and fair. Someone didn't think, "How can we make this experience better for our guests? What can we give them to make up for what we've had to take away? What about including real china and silverware and a cloth napkin so a guest can serve themselves? How about something sweet: a cookie or a beautifully wrapped chocolate truffle that they hadn't ordered?" It never ceases to astound me how a simple, almost-no-cost opportunity like this to please a customer is overlooked. You don't want your customer to be thinking about what they're missing. That's not the kind of attention you're looking for.

I like to think of my clients and their comfort the way I think of my guests at a dinner party. After my guests RSVP, I text and ask if anyone has any allergies or dietary restrictions and plan my menu accordingly. When my guests arrive, I've done all the work to ensure that they have a pleasant evening. The candles are lit, the house is tidy, the table is set, music is playing, the food is prepared. In the powder room I've lit a fragrant candle and folded the toilet paper into a V. I wash my face, change into a fresh shirt, and comb my hair. I put ice in the ice bucket and nuts or other snacks on the coffee table. Now I can focus 100 percent on being the consummate host.

I was once staying at a luxury hotel in Santa Barbara. Because of flight delays from New York, I got to my room at 2:00 a.m. I was tired, thirsty, and hungry. I opened up the minibar and it was empty except for a note that read, "We understand you have your preferred choices. Kindly contact your butler and he'll happily stock the minibar for you." That's a lot of bullshit. At that price point, why should I have to call at 2:00 a.m. — assuming there was someone available — and go through a list of what I wanted and wait for it to be delivered?

I had called the hotel to tell them I was going to be arriving late. Some hotels will email you before your arrival with options; why didn't they? The person who answered when I called could have asked if I wanted anything special in the bar at that point and passed that information along. Or they could have reasoned that I probably didn't want a burger when I arrived, but I still might appreciate finding a snack or some fruit and herbal tea in the room, along with a note that the butler would contact me in the morning. That would have been proactive thinking. They could have stocked the bar with a couple of bags of quality potato chips, the best chocolate bar, a granola bar, bottled water, mini bottles of scotch or vodka, and a half bottle of champagne or wine. Accommodating my preferences can wait until the morning. A less expensive hotel could put a cup of instant ramen noodles and breakfast biscuits beside the coffee maker. Even a thoughtfully stocked vending machine with a balance of sweet, savory, and healthful options tells your customer you've thought about what they might want or need.

●

## Make Data Work for You

You can, and should, ask your customer for information. To deliver the gold standard of customer service, you need as much data as you can get; *data is a powerful tool that will help you get attention*. People are now more willing to pass on information than ever before. Although they may not want to give you their year of birth, most people have no problem giving you the month and date. As the day approaches, you could offer them a discount on your product, or a gift with purchase. How about a ten-minute foot massage if they book a pedicure? Remember when you were hesitant to give a credit card number over the phone or online? Now, we Americans do 70 to 80 percent of our shopping online and don't think twice about making a onetime payment on a site we may never use again.

Asking is how you find out what they want, what's important to them, what you're doing right, and what you can do better. Everybody is looking for feedback. When I get home from a doctor's appointment, there's a survey waiting for me in my email. How long did I wait before I saw the doctor? Was I greeted when I walked in? Did the doctor take my concerns seriously? Did she explain things clearly? When I go to the drugstore, I get a survey: Could I find everything I was looking for? Was the store clean?

It's up to you to connect the dots. If you're selling a product—clothes, makeup, computer equipment—you have a record of customer purchases. If they've made a reservation at your restaurant, you have their name, their email address, and their phone number. Maybe they made a special request—it's someone's birthday or anniversary. (Note that so you can invite them back next year.) If they're checking into your hotel, you have all their information and their address. If they're a member of a loyalty club, they may have given you information on their preferences: what kind of room they prefer, whether they want to be near or away from the elevator, whether they travel with their pet, their interests, favorite destinations, dietary preferences, whether they're a runner or a museumgoer.

I know someone who wanted a Pepsi on his flight to Paris; the airline didn't use that brand. He tweeted about his disappointment. When he arrived at his hotel, there was a Pepsi waiting for him in his room, chilling in an ice bucket. Some people might think that sounds a little creepy. I think it was smart. The guest put the information out on social media, and the hotel acted on it. Social media is social. It's public information.

*Use that data*. If you can afford it, you can commission a custom piece of software, unique to your business and your needs. If you don't have the money, you can create an Excel spreadsheet or a Word document or use your computer's calendar or reminder function. I want to come up with an app that tracks clients' life events. For example, we have a client who has an eleven-year-old grandson. We know that in less than a year she's going to be involved in planning his bar mitzvah; we should touch base with her around that time. We see on Instagram that a client's daughter just got engaged; a congratulatory note or email can start a discussion about wedding plans. If you check your records and see that Company X hasn't refilled an order for paper towels in six months, they might be buying from someone else. Why not send an email suggesting it's time to reorder? You'll provide expedited rather than standard shipping at the same cost. It's all about making the experience about *them*.

I love to ask questions, and I've found that people love to talk about themselves. I want to find out as much as I can about each of my clients and what's important to them so I can create an event that is meaningful to *them*. I want to know what their favorite color is and their favorite flavor. Do they have a favorite vacation destination? What's their favorite restaurant? Have they hosted an event like this before? Attended one? What did they like? What didn't they like? As I design an event, I always ask the client to share with the team what they *dislike* as well as what they like so we can tailor elements that are reflections of their tastes.

●

## Consistency Is the Key

Consistency is key when you're providing the gold standard of customer service. Your customer wants to be confident they will get a consistent product or experience every time they come to you. Without standards and consistency, you can't deliver the goods and you have zero credibility. This isn't just a question of price point. It's one of the reasons McDonald's is so successful; a Big Mac and crispy fries will taste the same whether you're in North Dakota or Florida. Your customer wants to feel confident that you have their best interests at heart and that you'll be honest and forthcoming when you deal with them, even if it means telling them something they don't want to hear. Trust me, it's no fun telling a bride that if she spends 30 percent of her budget on her dress we can't give her the flowers she wants, or that the venue she had set her heart set on isn't available.

The gold standard of customer service means making your customer feel as special and appreciated the fifth time they visit your restaurant, store, or website as they do the first time. At Colin Cowie Lifestyle, that begins with assigning one producer and one designer to each client—and they're with that client from the first meeting to the end of their event. It means that the client gets the same gracious welcome at every meeting; they're served the beverages they prefer and snacks on good china and starched linen every time. It makes them feel familiar and comfortable.

If you're selling a product, simply saying thank you after a sale is made in person or online—no matter how small—is an easy but effective way to acknowledge that you appreciate your customer. Think about the last time that you got out of an Uber. Before you closed the door, there was an opportunity to rate the driver, give feedback on the driver's service delivery, and even offer a tip, should you want to. (Uber drivers rate our behavior as well; it's a two-way street.) Loyalty cards—for every ten drinks you get a free one—or giving a regular customer a bottle of her favorite polish so she can touch up a chipped nail at home, are thoughtful and not terribly expensive ways to reward loyalty and encourage repeat business. Since these little rewards are more common today, you need to go one step further and be sure you are the ones tracking, reminding, and giving them. If a customer is eligible and you keep quiet, thinking, "Well, they didn't add the code," you're not being proactive and you're not delivering the best customer experience!

The gold standard of customer service means offering your customer the unexpected. During the aftermath of COVID-19, with air travel down almost 50 percent, the airlines eliminated change fees to encourage people to get back in the air again and announced the change would be permanent. At a hotel it could mean having multilingual staff at the front desk, including someone who, like the young woman in the Marriott commercial, speaks American Sign Language. If you're an accountant or tax attorney, it could be offering a cup of tea, and remembering that your customer likes Earl Grey without sugar every time he comes in, and whether he wants music in the background or quiet while you're meeting. It takes the edge off a high-stress situation. It's easy to make someone feel great. Going for a treatment on his birthday at Memorial Sloan Kettering, a friend's husband was greeted with "Happy Birthday!" by every staff member he met with. Did it make him better? No. Did it make him *feel* better? It certainly helped.

Here's what not to do: become complacent, or make your customers feel like you don't value them or their time. If you really want to keep your customers' attention, you have to be quicker than your competitors. Our time has become more and more precious. Paradoxically, it is the one thing that doesn't cost anything, but it makes the biggest difference in your customers' experience. For example, I have a doctor who is consistently forty-five minutes late for our appointments. Every time. The last time I saw him, I called before I left my office and asked if the doctor was running on time. I was told yes, but when I arrived I waited for, yes, forty-five minutes. I went up to the receptionist and told her that when I had called I was told the doctor was on time, and yet I'd been waiting for forty-five minutes. Her response? "This is how it is here." Because he's not part of a bigger practice, or associated with a practice in a hospital, there's no one to keep him or his staff accountable for the way his office is managed.

In my business, I know that if someone has emailed me to discuss an event, they've emailed five other companies. We used to respond to inquiries that came in over the weekend on Monday morning. Now we respond within hours. If a call comes in during the day, it's returned within half an hour because I believe that the first person who contacts you is the one who gets the job more than 90 percent of the time.

This also goes for any kind of customer communication. Your customer is the one who gets to determine what's urgent and what's not. If your customer has a question or a problem, waiting twenty-four hours for an answer may be too long. They need and want your attention now. You may feel that's a reasonable amount of time, but in an age of instant messaging and online chat, your customer may not. If you're a small company and don't have the staff to deliver 24/7 customer service, you can set up an automatic reply to queries letting them know when to expect an answer. If you can respond sooner, you've exceeded their expectations. (You can also be too aggressive. I recently ordered a chair online. Before the chair was delivered, I'd received a phone call, a text, and an email asking me how I like my new purchase. Clearly the company's internal communication, as well as their customer communication, could use some fine tuning.) I never forget what Sam Walton said: "There is only one boss—the customer. And he can fire everybody in the company from the chairman on down, simply by spending his money elsewhere."

What you don't want is for your customer to feel like they're getting an automated, Dear Fill-in-the-Blank response. I had a cable issue and went to the website. When I couldn't find an answer in the FAQs, I activated the chat feature and laid out my problem. After two responses, it was clear that I was dealing with a bot who couldn't actually help. I had no recourse because the cable company is essentially a monopoly. Do I feel good about dealing with them? No. Would I change companies if I could? Yes. If you're not the cable company, your customer has choices. When they think you are listening and care about their concerns, they'll choose you over your competition.

## Whatever It Takes

The gold standard of customer service means graduating from the University of Whatever It Takes. At a wedding in Malibu Canyon, the van with floral headpieces for the flower girls was stuck in LA traffic and obviously wasn't going to make it to the venue on time for the ceremony. I was standing under an arbor constructed of 450,000 Ecuadorean roses; a few dozen wouldn't be missed. I took some roses from the arbor's back side and was able to hastily make beautiful headpieces for the girls; no one was the wiser. Then there was the time a bride said to me, "I hate this veil. I wanted something that was more bohemian." I asked if she wanted me to help with it and she said yes. The guests were walking into the ceremony while I was reworking the veil with a pair of scissors and tape. She loved it, and walked down the aisle a happy bride.

I have learned that when a client says they will take care of an element of the wedding, I should become wary. On one occasion, the client was supposed to supply the wedding cake; they were supposed to bring it to the venue on their private plane. They took off and left the cake behind. I called one of my producers. She purchased two first-class tickets to Hawaii and arranged to have someone from the cake shop deliver the cake to her husband at the airport. He and the cake boarded the plane and made it to Hawaii in time for the wedding. Flying a cake to Hawaii may seem extreme, but the gold standard of customer service means doing whatever it takes!

There was the time I was producing a royal wedding in Doha. Our client's staff told us that they were providing gifts of scarves for the two thousand guests, and there was nothing we needed to do except put a gift at each place setting. At midday on the wedding day, we discovered that the scarves had not been wrapped. We had the gifts, the wrapping (thank goodness), a large waitstaff, and a few hours. We jumped into action and assigned each team member and waiter a designated number of scarves. All the scarves were at the place settings by the time the guests sat down to dinner. It's up to us to pay attention, even if our customer does not.

In his bestselling book *The Checklist Manifesto: How to Get Things Right*, surgeon Atul Gawande points out that in an increasingly complex world, when we fail, it's usually because we haven't made use of what we know. It's easy to skip a step or forget to ask the right question or fail to account for every eventuality. Sometimes even when you think you have thought of everything, you're surprised and have to act in the moment.

There was the wedding in Maui that was jeopardized by an unexpected hurricane. Our creative partners on-site threatened to walk off the job. My team researched every other possibility to move the wedding from an outdoor tent into a ballroom. The bride was devastated at the thought of having to move her wedding inside. I couldn't let this happen. I convinced the creative partners to stay by housing them overnight and giving them a food and beverage allowance. I took a calculated but necessary risk to ensure the success of the event: I guaranteed we would pay for any equipment that might be lost, if in fact, the hurricane hit. Our bottom line would have taken a temporary hit, but it was more important to keep my promise and my reputation intact. In the end, the hurricane never made landfall and our bride was able to have the wedding of her dreams.

Sometimes you may think an event will be straightforward, but I always expect the unexpected. We were doing a wedding on a private island in Bora Bora; it was a forty-five-minute boat ride from the main island. Our two on-site concierges arrived a few days ahead of the event to familiarize themselves with the property and discovered that the new chef had not brought in provisions for the forty guests who were soon to arrive. My team took their boat to the local market and bought everything they could, then reached out to local hotels to help supplement their supplies. Thank goodness we thought to send staff ahead of time. We have done that with events at remote venues ever since.

•

## Be Prepared—For Anything

In our office, managing uncertainty and preventing errors day-to-day starts with a twenty-five-page illustrated document detailing procedures and protocols on exactly how the office space should be managed by our team. It covers everything from day-to-day maintenance of our kitchen space and how to set up the conference room for a meeting to how our clients are welcomed. I'm a big believer in "a place for everything and everything in its place" because it saves time and makes *everyone's* life easier.

When we book an event, we start a master checklist that is constantly reviewed and updated. It covers everything from creating a client information sheet to post-event follow up, including thank-you notes to our staff and creative partners. We also create a book for each event that has information on every aspect of the party including keyed plans that show what the floral centerpieces look like, how the tables are arranged, how they are set, and what china, glassware, and silver are used. It's literally a day-by-day, minute-by-minute timeline. I call it our Bible, and it's essential when there are so many detailed elements that create one magical moment. For a multi-day event, the volume can run to more than a hundred pages. Everyone involved in the event gets a copy and is in constant communication during the event, with everyone working towards the same goal: to create the ultimate guest experience.

Many companies only focus on customer service when things go wrong, rather than setting up an empowered corporate culture that encourages creativity and caring and anticipates the unforeseen. It's one thing to land the account or get the order. It's another to deliver an exceptional customer experience. Mistakes happen—a restaurant loses a reservation, the hotel room isn't ready on time, a package arrives damaged. In the middle of planning a three-day overseas event, the producer takes another job. (I'll talk more about mistakes and how to recover from them later in the book.)

We once had an extremely high-profile client from Hong Kong who was getting married in Australia to avoid paparazzi. They even flew to another country first to throw the paparazzi off their trail, but it didn't work. Within hours of our client's arrival at the hotel, there were fifty photographers and reporters following their every move. Realizing there was no avoiding the publicity, after consulting with our client we decided to create a welcoming environment for the press, knowing that their reporting would be more favorable if we accommodated them. We created designated press parking and holding areas, provided lighting, and even meals. We scheduled access for them around each of the weekend's nine events. By accommodating the press while at the same time setting clear boundaries, we were able to control the situation and give our client the experience they wanted with minimal disruption.

A smart organization takes the time to look for all the points where something could go wrong—the receptionist forgets to enter a reservation, a package could be mislabeled, a hotel guest departs late—and comes up with procedures and alternatives to address the problems before they occur. Like the swan who appears to be gliding effortlessly on the surface of the lake, but is paddling furiously underneath, you are in control and do the work before a problem occurs so your customer can be focused on your product or service, and their experience.

KEEP IN MIND:

- Your customer has their choice of products and services. You want them to choose yours. If they can't find you, they can't buy your product or service.
- Know your market. See what your competitors are doing, look at what you're losing, and put all of that information to use to increase your market share.
- Make data work for you. You need as much data as you can get from your customer: *data is a powerful tool that will help you get attention*.
- Consistency is key. Your customer wants to be confident they will get a consistent product or experience every time they come to you.
- The gold standard of customer service requires creativity and flexibility. Be prepared for any eventuality and to do whatever it takes to deliver on your promise.

NOW ASK YOURSELF:

- Am I doing enough to get, and keep, my potential customers' attention?
- How many new opportunities can I find to engage with my customer?
- Does my customer receive the same level of service every time they interact with me or my team?

# two

*Serving Up
an Unforgettable
Customer Experience*

T he best customer experience is consistent, personalized, authentic, luxurious, timely, and for the customer, effortless. Guaranteeing a great customer experience should be SOP, standard operating procedure. You can make it part of your company's DNA.

Every customer deserves respectful and caring service when they interact with you or your team, no matter what service or product you provide, and no matter how much or how little they contribute to the bottom line. You never know whether the purchase of a single T-shirt could lead to a relationship worth thousands of dollars. You can't have that kind of consistency without standards of service that are applied to every customer in every interaction.

It may seem counterintuitive, but companywide standards applied to every customer interaction result in personalized

service. For example, before a new client arrives for a meeting or appointment, do you and your associates or team
members try to get as much information as you can during
an initial phone call so you all can prepare content that will
resonate with the prospective client? You can easily do a
brief internet search for a photo of the client so that whoever
is greeting them will instantly recognize them when they
arrive at your office. You might assign one team member to
meet them in the lobby at the elevator. One person we know
of calls that job "Director of First Impressions." That person
can then comfortably greet them by name and say, "It's a
pleasure to meet you, Mr. Kent and Ms. Jackson," instead of
"*Are* you Mr. Kent and Ms. Jackson?" In the conference room
you could have a custom slide show on the monitor with the
customers' names, a printout of the meeting agenda, or a
sample display of your product. At every step of the way, you
are saying you are prepared. You then offer a selection of
beverages: water, of course, perhaps a choice of still or spar-
kling, a lemon or lime wedge. You might also have coffee,
espresso drinks, and tea available. Using real glasses, real
china cups, and cloth napkins sets the tone of the meeting:
your prospective customers or clients immediately become
your guests and get to experience your thoughtful hospitality. That's the way we do it at Colin Cowie Lifestyle, with a
few additional flourishes: There are always fresh flowers or a
flowering orchid plant. As they leave the meeting, each client
receives a gift bag with a handwritten note to say thank you
for coming to our offices today, and we send a follow-up note
two days later. A gift doesn't have to be expensive, but it
should represent your brand, and establish a connection between you and your customer. We do this with every new
customer, making the experience not just a luxurious one,
but also a personal one.

It's essential to get together with your group before the meeting and brainstorm about the best way you might establish a rapport with your new clients and use those strategies to cement that relationship with future meetings. Every client's expectations are different. It's up to you to anticipate their expectations and instead of just meeting those expectations, surpass them.

Staying at a hotel in Hong Kong, I once left an expensive watch on the night table when I went out for dinner. While I was out, one of the hotel team texted me a picture of the watch, explaining that the housekeeper who had entered the room to perform the nightly turndown service had taken the liberty of placing it in the hotel safe. In fact, at this hotel, I trusted that I could leave my watch out while I was not in my room, and the housekeeper's actions reinforced that trust.

## The Handwritten Note

ONE OF THE EASIEST WAYS to serve up a memorable customer service experience and make a personal connection with your client is to send a handwritten note or card. Few people write notes anymore, and that's why getting one is a nice surprise that makes a noticeable emotional impression. In descending order from most to least impact is the timely handwritten note, an immediate phone call, an email, and a text. Today, when thank-yous and even condolences are sent via email and text, there's almost nothing that takes so little effort on your part and goes such a long way toward making a good impression. What does it cost you? A nice notecard, a stamp, and a few minutes of your time. What's the return on that investment? Priceless.

There are some companies that have embraced the power of the personal note, and a number of those don't sell luxury products. Online pet product company Chewy.com will send a handwritten condolence message to grieving pet parents, for example. Apple Hill Farm, a small alpaca farm in North Carolina that sells yarn and other wool products, and Long Winter Soap, a family business in Maine that sells small-batch soaps and body products, both include handwritten thank-yous on preprinted cards with every order.

A writer for *Inc.* flew to New York on Delta during the 2020 pandemic, when flights were almost empty. Before the plane landed, a flight attendant gave each passenger a handwritten note, thanking them for flying with Delta and for their loyalty. It wasn't just the content of the note that impressed the writer, it was the fact that it was handwritten and personalized. He says, and I agree: "Every time you interact with a customer you have an opportunity to reinforce your values and build the relationship . . . every effort you make to reach out to your customers . . . is a big deal."

When I go through my pile of mail, I inevitably gravitate toward the handwritten pieces. I love cards and stationery. I prefer stationery of extra thick cardstock and personalized with my initials. I have matching lined envelopes with my address printed on the flap. You can find a variety of quality paper products from high end to less expensive almost anywhere, and of course online. Remember, with a handwritten note it's the thought that counts—not the cost of the stationery or pen you used. I find it useful to keep a supply of my personalized notecards and stamps on my desk at home and at work. When I travel, I take some with me, setting myself up to do the right thing no matter where I am. I stock up on cards before I need them—blank and for specific occasions—at my favorite store so I have an appropriate card for a birthday, a housewarming, or to say congratulations. I suggest you do the same; having cards on hand means it's more likely that you'll send one in a timely way when the occasion arises.

There's almost no occasion where a handwritten note isn't appropriate. If I've gone out to dinner with someone, when I get home I go straight to my desk. If I'm still a little tipsy, I have lots of adjectives on the tip of my tongue. I write a thank-you note. Here's an example:

*Dear Peter,*

*Thank you for including us in your kind invitation last night. I had the best time! Dinner was beyond delicious as was the interesting company. I look forward to reciprocating in the next couple of weeks.*

*Much love,*
*Colin*

The next morning it gets popped in the mail. When I receive a gift or someone has done something nice for me, I write a note. If I see an article in a newspaper or magazine that is of interest to a friend or client, I clip it and send it with a note, or if I've seen something online, I may print it out and forward it. As Jack Ezon of Embark Beyond, a luxury lifestyle and travel advisory service, noted, in a world oversaturated with digital content, print rises above the digital noise. It stands out. I like to send a physical copy (and because so few people do, it does make an impression), but an email or text with an attachment or photo works too. Either way, your friend or client will remember that you were thinking of them.

Because I travel so much, often scouting for event venues, when I arrive in the hotel, hotel management knows me. The general manager will graciously upgrade my room and send an amenity, like a fruit basket or bottle of wine. In response, I write a handwritten note, attach my business card, and hand it to the front desk, like this one:

*Dear Sharon,*

*Thank you for making me so welcome at the hotel and for the
fabulous bottle of Bordeaux; it was most welcome after such a
long trip. I sincerely appreciate your giving me a room with
such a lovely view. I had a great time and look forward to
staying with you the next time I visit Palm Beach.*

*Best wishes always,*
*Colin.*

I've now created a more personal and emotional connection
with the general manager, paving the way for a more personalized experience. And who knows, possibly an upgrade! If the
concierge has gone out of his way for me, I'll put a gratuity into
a notecard to say thank you. Try doing this too. It's a way of making a positive memorable impression, and most assuredly, you'll
be on their radar the next time you make a reservation, need
their assistance, or ask for advice. It feels good to give, and also
to receive.

You don't have to overthink it. Your clients aren't judging you
on the quality of your prose. All it takes is two or three lines,
written legibly (print if you have to), sent in a timely way, to create
a lasting, personal, and positive, connection.

## Do You See Your Customer?

At Memorial Sloan Kettering Cancer Center, one of the first
questions a patient is asked is "What do you want to be called?"
Not what's your full name, or the name on your insurance
card, but what do *you* want to be called. That simple question
makes a world of difference by acknowledging the patient

isn't just a patient, but an individual in their most vulnerable moment. Your customer wants to be seen and heard; if one medical facility has the attitude of "Show up and shut up" and another takes the time to discuss treatment options and listen to a patient's concerns without dismissing them, where is that patient more likely to go? If you treat your customer like they are not important to you, *even if it's unintentional*, they will go, or want to go, somewhere else. Admittedly, I've been guilty of this. We had a very difficult client, and I let her get to me, instead of dealing directly with the problem. The rest of the team picked up on my disdain, and it affected their interactions with her. We lost the client and the fee. Your reactions are transmitted to your team. I've learned from this experience that it's better to deal with issues as they arise. It sends a strong message to your team as well as to your client.

Identifying and understanding your core customer is essential to delivering the best customer experience. I like to say, "You can't please everyone. You're not champagne." What do you really know about your customer? Do they prefer being called by their nickname rather than their "real" name or a more formal form of address? Do they prefer their coffee after dessert, their shirts hung and not starched, or the color pink? Are they price-sensitive? Are they interested in fine dining or farm-to-table?

There's no algorithm or rigid formula for creating a personal customer experience; whether you're selling to a broad demographic or an individual, what's important to your client must be important to you. As I suggested earlier, when we're courting a client, we arm ourselves with as much information as possible before we meet. We put ourselves in our customer's shoes and ask:

What do we think would make us (as our customer) happy? Theirs is the most important point of view.

What kind of experience do we think they would like to have?

And then:

What would our competition do if they knew what we were doing?

Do that. And have fun doing it.

Each time you are selling your client your product or service, are you aware of what they're looking for and what moves them? What's their passion? Often that involves reading between the lines of what they tell you to intuit what they really want. In my business, I've found that clients who are over forty take a more traditional approach; they want to be presented in the best light to their guests, family, and friends.

My younger clients are less concerned about what's "right" or traditional and more interested in expressing their individuality in their event. They want to know if we're eco-friendly, if we leave a low carbon footprint, and that we actively give back. How do I know? When I meet with a client, at the beginning of the meeting I let them do the talking. My curious nature makes it easy for me to ask questions. Some are straightforward requests for information: Do you prefer plated service or food stations? Formal or informal? Mediterranean or New American? Would you prefer that we communicate by email? Text? Do you prefer physical copies of forms and information or digital only? What's your favorite food or ingredient? Your least favorite? Others are to elicit more information about who my client is: What's your favorite color? Do you have a memory associated with that? What do you like to do? Where do you like to travel when you go on vacation? What was the most exciting thing you've done on vacation? Is there something you'd like to do that you haven't done yet?

You start to build a profile of the individual, which helps you paint a picture that will appeal to them. After every meeting with a client, we debrief as a team, and every interaction with the client going forward is informed by what we've learned. That's the kind of attention to personal preferences and detail that can set you apart and can make a difference between a potential client choosing you or choosing your competitor.

Every customer wants to know that not only do you stand behind your product or service, but that there is some real meat on the bone behind your action and that they believe that you will make things right if something goes wrong. (I'll talk more about this and the fine art of the apology in chapter 6.) If you don't, you lose faith and credibility, and that customer. One of the most gratifying compliments I ever received from a client (and it came from Oprah, so it meant a great deal to me) was that she knew nothing bad would ever happen at a Colin Cowie event. If your client doesn't trust you and your product, it doesn't matter if you have an amazing product. There's nothing more frustrating than loving something and being disappointed in how and when it's delivered, or how a problem with the product or delivery is dealt with; it's even more upsetting if you've talked to others about how wonderful your initial experience was and are now embarrassed that you did so. That's why even if your product isn't the best in its field, you can still build customer loyalty with the gold standard of customer service.

No matter how carefully orchestrated and artfully scripted your policy, if your customer doesn't feel the experience is authentic—if there's not an emotional connection—they will look elsewhere. It's very much about delivering the *right* service, in the right amounts, at the right time for that customer. There can be nothing automatic or preprogrammed about this interaction; be aware of what your customer's body language, tone of voice, or response to your outreach is telling you, and act accordingly. Sometimes there's a fine line between service that makes a person feel appreciated and cared for and service that becomes annoying or invasive. It could be too many texts or emails, or too many requests for reviews. At a brick-and-mortar store, an aggressive salesperson who shadows a browsing customer can drive them right out of the building as quickly—or more quickly!—than one who is unavailable or even rude. We each have our own thresholds of too little or too much, and it's up to you to get as much information about their preferences as quickly as possible. Find the right amounts for each particular customer.

An example of what *not* to do is an experience I had on vacation at a high-end spa in a well-known five-star hotel on the Mexican Riviera. When I arrived, I appreciated the attentiveness of the staff, but within the first couple of hours I was approached almost twenty times by different people asking, "How are you, Mr. Cowie?" "Can I get you anything, Mr. Cowie?" "Are you enjoying yourself, Mr. Cowie?" By the tenth interruption, the incessant questions started to feel programmed rather than sincere expressions of concern and became an intrusion into my Zen space. The spa experience itself was eclipsed by the constant interruptions. I felt like my personal space was being invaded. And when a spa attendant got onto all fours in an attempt to put my slippers on me, I thought, "Enough!" What was supposed to be a luxurious experience quickly went from pampering to annoying. But let me make this clear: This was not the staff's fault. They were clearly following a protocol they'd been trained—not educated—to use.

•

## Customer Service Is the New Luxury

In my opinion the definition of luxury has changed as the economy has risen and fallen. Consumer habits and behavior patterns are changing, and what used to be thought of as luxury is not that luxurious anymore. We're seeing the mass production of luxury as brands that used to be associated with a unique, and often handmade, product—a bag, a dress, a jacket—have become examples of vertical integration and profit centers.

Luxury used to be something that came in an orange Hermès box tied with a saddle-stitched brown ribbon. It was exclusive and it was expensive. You couldn't buy it easily; you had to go to a particular store—or at one point, to a particular country. Today you can buy orange boxes in airports and train stations. You can find them online; in fact, there's almost nothing you can think of that you can't find on a website and have delivered incredibly quickly to anywhere in the world.

On the plus side, luxury has become much more democratic. The combination of the global economy and increased competition means that a consumer is looking for immediate delivery and quality at the right price. When what you want and what you can get align, it feels luxurious. If you can give your customer a great experience buying or using your product, it's a luxury experience.

After moving to a new apartment, I bought a California King bed and was looking forward to treating myself to a new blanket. As I don't buy blankets very often, I wanted to invest in a good quality blanket, and perhaps indulge myself. Blankets are easy to find online, and in my search, I found a wide variety of cashmere offerings available. (Now that's treating yourself, isn't it?) Prices ranged from $300 all the way to

$7,000. I was able to find a fabulous site, JG Switzer. It was beautiful; it was elegant; it was luxe; it navigated wonderfully. It was very easy to find what I was looking for, and ordering was seamless.

A few days later, I received a big cardboard box. I opened the box and inside was a beautifully sealed, plastic envelope. I removed the plastic and inside was a black canvas bag (summer storage for the blanket) with a zipper on three sides. I easily removed the bag, unzipped it, and found a gorgeous, silk camel-and-black striped bag with two button ties on the top. I untied them and opened up the striped bag. Then there was something that took me by surprise: a note from the person who packaged it. A beautifully *handwritten* note. Seriously? I took my finger and rubbed the ink; it *was* handwritten, not printed. I opened the bag and there was *my* blanket, tied with a four-inch-wide satin ribbon. It was an amazing experience. I couldn't wait to unfold the blanket and put it on my bed!

I could have ordered a less expensive blanket, or one of equal quality from another website. But I might not have had the same effortless, pleasurable, luxurious, personalized interaction. No matter what I spent on the blanket, it was worth it to me for the experience I had buying it and unwrapping it when it arrived at my home. The website stated clearly that if there had been a problem it would be taken care of properly. I knew there would not have been an issue if I wanted to return the merchandise because I wasn't pleased with my purchase or it had been damaged in transit.

When I bought my blanket, I felt taken care of and that the seller was concerned about how I felt; that's true luxury. It doesn't matter what you're selling. If your customer has had a great experience, if you surprise them by including a value-added extra that had never crossed their mind or meeting an unanticipated desire, that's luxury. It's the feeling that all your senses are in harmony, and you don't feel like anything else is required; that your every need — even the ones you didn't know you had — are being taken care of. These key elements of constant surprise and feeling satisfied continually strengthen the bond between you and your customer. Simply purchasing a beautiful blanket that I enjoy and know will last for years gave me the experience of feeling I was giving myself the gift I really wanted. And their extra surprises made it such a memorable experience that I'm now writing to you about it!

There's no reason that even the most mundane and everyday experiences can't meet the definition of luxury. When I'm made to feel valued and special in a place I least expect it, like a taxi or car service, it's actually a heightened experience. In New York, for decades the yellow medallion taxi was the only game in town. The cabs were often dirty with torn upholstery, and they and their drivers sometimes stank of smoke and greasy food. In summer, cabs were often not air-conditioned or out of freon. They wouldn't take you to Brooklyn or Queens or Harlem. If you told them you didn't want to talk, or asked them to turn off the music, you didn't expect the drivers to be pleasant, and often they weren't. Then came Uber and Lyft, the disrupters. They weren't just competing with the Yellow Cabs; they were competing with each other. The cars were clean and there were mints and bottles of water in the back seat. There was a connection, and often a cable for you to charge your phone. Some drivers would get out of the car, open the door for you, and help you with your bags of purchases or luggage. They changed the playing ground completely, and as a result, cab drivers are a whole lot sweeter today because they know you have other choices. The new car services created a proactive environment of anticipating your wants and addressing your possible needs for those few minutes in their vehicle. The everyday experience of getting from one place to another has changed for the better.

Another example is the gas station a friend of mine frequents. It's not the most convenient in town, but they still use attendants, which is unusual where she lives. You don't have to get out of your car in bad weather. The young men who work there greet you with a "good morning" or "good afternoon," and say "thank you" when they hand you back your credit card. When the owner isn't busy, he'll come over and say hello, and thank you for your business. People go out of their way to get gas from his business because he makes them feel appreciated. Identifying the things that people really value in a commercial experience is key to making the connection with customers or clients.

Some people think that having unlimited choices is luxurious. I disagree! We're on information overload all the time. Access to excess isn't that exciting anymore. I don't want to spend my time doing someone else's job. For example, there was a restaurant that was the epitome of that kind of overwhelming choice. You'd order steak and be presented with a choice of nine ridiculously expensive cuts of meat and twelve steak knives. The binder that held the wine list was two inches thick and boasted four hundred wines to choose from. When it was time to sign the check, you'd be presented with five different pens. I spend all day making decisions. When I go out to dinner, I don't want a four-page menu. I don't want to have to work to enjoy my dinner. I'm much happier with five or six carefully curated choices, thank you!

•

## Great Service Comes from Ruthless Editing

Great style and great service come from ruthless editing; luxury and good business today is getting rid of the 90 percent that doesn't belong and keeping the 10 percent that does. It's why websites like Rank & Style or *New York* magazine's feature *The Strategist* are popular; they take the work out of sifting through thousands of choices to curate the best ones. Even Amazon has begun curating personalized choices for us.

Timing is so incredibly important. At Colin Cowie Lifestyle, when we get a customer inquiry, we know that person is already in shopping mode. It's the same with any business or service provider. We're not so conceited to think that we're the only person that they reached out to. We know that our potential customer is talking to five other people. All of us could be saying pretty much the same thing, at least in the beginning. The person who responds to the call first has a foot in the door; if I'm the first person to strike up a conversation with you, I have the first opportunity to create a positive emotional connection. That can give me an advantage when you're ready to make a decision.

Waiting for anything is not luxury. Period. Your customer can make you wait for their decision, or an appointment, but you can never make your customer wait for you. There was a time that you'd wait for a letter in the mail. Then you were standing by the fax machine. Now your phone is glued to your hand and you can get information in two seconds. There's technology in the works that will make information acquisition even faster. We've become way more impatient. Time is money, for both you and your customer. An ecommerce site needs to be easy to navigate and instantly responsive to keep a user engaged. If you have a restaurant, no one should wait to see a waitperson, receive a menu, or have their water glasses filled. If your customer is looking for a salesperson and can't find one right away, or the checkout line is too long, they're likely to walk out the door. (Trader Joe's in New York City and Joe's Stone Crab in Miami Beach seem to be exceptions to this. I don't know why.)

I was invited to the opening of a very trendy, very expensive new hotel in Times Square. The invitation said to prepare for the unexpected, and the time on the invitation was 10:00 p.m. After waiting outside for forty-five minutes in thirty-five-degree weather, I went from a feeling of anticipation to being simply annoyed, and I left. I wrote the hosts a note explaining why I had left. They could easily have invited me for a private tour at a later time, but I never received a response. That was a missed opportunity for them, because I enjoy being able to recommend and support an exciting new hotel. Why put my foot in that hotel again, or recommend it to friends and clients?

Twenty-five years ago, you could get people to wait in line to create a big buzz and make your place feel exclusive, but now it's bad business. It's rude and inappropriate. There are many other places to go where you will get a warm welcome. Your customers, like me, want to feel valued and loved! Waiting five, or in this case, even fifteen minutes is reasonable, and can increase our anticipation, but the customer's patience for an extended wait has diminished considerably with our ability to have, and our expectation of, swift gratification. We work hard for every dollar, and we want someone to feel that they have earned our choice to spend our money with them. Ultimately, we enjoy places where we feel our time and experience is valued. That's why I insist that we start the weddings we produce no more than fifteen minutes past invitation time. We value our guests' time, and making a good first impression is important to setting the tone for the rest of the evening.

Luxury should feel effortless to your customer. They don't want to worry about whether an order will arrive on time or if pieces will be missing, and it's not necessary that they see the machine behind the scenes that makes this happen. Anticipation and prevention are two of the most valuable tools in your toolbox that will allow you to refine and curate the customer experience. (I'll talk more about that in a later chapter.) It's vital to strategize the preproduction work behind the scenes to make your service seamless. And let's be honest, it takes a lot of thought, planning, and work. Be like the furiously paddling swans I mentioned earlier, who appear to glide effortlessly past the beautiful water lilies. That effortlessness is all your client needs to see.

●

## Always Go Above and Beyond

When you invite someone to come to your home for dinner or are making a presentation, you're expected to be well prepared. If it's a dinner party, you don't answer the door in a dirty apron or set the table after your guests arrive. You don't serve pasta to a guest who's gluten-free or roast beef to your vegetarian uncle. You don't go into a meeting without thinking ahead. You don't make a presentation without practicing speaking from your notes or show up late.

If I'm presenting a budget for an event, I've done my research: I know what the costs for the food, décor, entertainment, flowers, and event space are. I try to anticipate every question or concern my client may have and have answers for them. It's enjoyable to bring up solutions to problems they may not know about or present questions that they may be reluctant to ask. You may not be able to think of every scenario, but you can brainstorm with your team to prepare and arm yourself with enough information so that you can easily navigate through unexpected circumstances.

Think of what went into making the computer you use every day: the coders, the designers, and the user experience professionals who put in—quite literally—millions of hours of work so you could simply turn on your computer and get to work. I love the story about Steve Jobs, who obsessed over a particular screw *inside* the Mac. When he was reminded that no one would know it was there, or how much thought and work went into getting it right, he said, "*I* know." Though that screw was invisible to the end user, it made a difference to Jobs, and ultimately, to the customer. The fact that it mattered to him makes me think that I, his customer, matter to him. They are looking out for me! It's why people are willing to pay a premium for Apple products. It doesn't matter whether the user experience is in the virtual world or in real life. In some ways I think the tech world is ahead in this; creating a seamless user experience, known as UX, is an important job. If your website or platform fails to deliver a positive UX, you fall behind.

Like the user who doesn't see the screw inside the Mac, my clients don't see the hundreds of elements that go into creating our unforgettable events. I prefer to call my external support teams creative partners, not vendors. Vendors sell hot dogs at the baseball stadium. My support teams are highly skilled artisans. We rely on our creative partners and suppliers to help us make that magic, and we look for people who will give us the same kind of exceptional service we give our clients.

Brion Shemeley of HITECH is one. He's a fabricator: he manufactures things like custom furniture and installations. He's one of the most proactive people I know. Typically, we have to give a fabricator explicit and detailed instructions before they can give us an estimate or put a project into production; Brion will build a prototype for a dance floor before we ask for it. When one of my producers was working on a vow renewal, she made a *very* rough sketch of a DJ booth on a napkin. Two days later, Brion sent an email with a detailed rendering, along with dimensions, finishes, and textures, asking if it was along the lines of what she was thinking. It happened to be exactly what she wanted. But even if it hadn't been, Brion's email would have jump-started the creative conversation.

Brion's business practices are also admirable. He knows his clients are often juggling multiple projects, and he manages up. If a team hasn't made a decision about a design, he'll send reminder emails that they're a week away from incurring a rush fee, then three days out, and then one day away. He sends reminders after he's sent a bill so clients can avoid paying a late fee.

Another example is Milk and Honey, a video production company. We had hired them to shoot a twenty-first birthday celebration. The party was on a Saturday night, and ran quite late. The next morning, all the guests awoke to find an email with a one-minute sizzle reel of the party. The videographers had identified the key players—the guest of honor, her boyfriend, her family, and closest friends—and featured them prominently. We hadn't asked them to do it, but the family and their guests (and we!) were delighted. The company had anticipated an unanticipated need.

Great customer service is more than the sum of its parts. If one of those elements—attention to detail, personalization, filter of elegance, teamwork, communication, consistency, or standards—is missing, or if one of your team isn't on board, you can't offer your customer what they're looking for. They won't have a reason to walk through your door or buy your product again.

It may feel like an overwhelming task to create the best customer experience, but you can start by dreaming big. It costs nothing to dream, and dreams and imagination have no limits. When you have that big picture in your mind, it becomes your North Star and will help guide every decision you make from beginning to end, bottom to top. Once you've imagined the best possible scenario, start small. One change can get the ball rolling, and build your momentum to transforming your future.

I always tell my clients that we like to dream big and then cut the cloth according to the size of the budget. One of our clients wanted something spectacular at his birthday party. I came up with the idea of projecting moving images from floor to ceiling on the walls of a soundstage, surrounding the guests with beautiful visual images and sound. It was an added expense, but by adjusting other elements of the budget, we were able to create an amazing guest experience and have a very happy client.

KEEP IN MIND:

- Great service comes from ruthless editing. The best customer service is consistent, personalized, authentic, timely, and appears effortless.
- Luxury no longer means elite. It's accessible and within everyone's reach. Customer service is the new luxury.
- Every customer is different, even when they can appear to want the same things. Don't presume to know *them*. Instead, presume to know the *choices* you think they would enjoy.

- Always go above and beyond. If you can't give your customer what they want, they can easily find someone else who will.

NOW ASK YOURSELF:

- How does this apply to me, our team, and our business?
- What do I see as the best customer experience for our product or service, and how can we better create that for our customer?
- What's the lowest hanging fruit: the one most obvious and easiest change you can make ASAP to meet that goal?
- The winning formula for proactive customer service is:
  1. Attention to detail, demonstrating excellence
  2. Personalization, creating the emotional connection
  3. Filter of elegance to elevate service
  4. Teamwork and communication, the brothers and sisters of success
  5. Standards and consistency: one depends on the other

# three

*Customer Service*

*Is the New Currency*

T here are two types of customer service: reactive and proactive. Reactive customer service is easy, and what most
businesses provide. *Proactive* service allows you to anticipate
the unanticipated needs of the customer.

Reactive customer service isn't enough to keep your customer from looking elsewhere. Probably 95 percent of companies give their clients reactive service. It corrects a situation
when something goes wrong but doesn't anticipate or prevent
a problem from happening or spiraling out of control: a room
isn't ready at check-in, the wrong item is delivered by mistake,
an order is late. These kinds of mistakes are easily corrected,
and you do win some customer loyalty. However, your customer has already been inconvenienced or annoyed, and their
opinion of your company and services has already been damaged or tarnished. Worst of all, when they talk about the

experience, they usually begin by emphasizing what went wrong, not how you fixed the problem.

On a business trip to Miami, I arranged for a rental car. I arrived at the airport and went to the pickup area to wait for the vehicle that would take me to the area where I could pick up my car. I waited ten minutes. I waited fifteen minutes more. I picked up the service phone and called the company to ask where my pickup was and was told that the van was already there. I said, "I'm standing here, and the van is not here. No van has stopped here." I reiterated exactly where I was, and he confirmed that I was in the right spot. Thirty minutes went by. I called again and was told the van was coming. Forty-five minutes went by. I called again and said, "I'm doing my best to be a gentleman and I'm doing my best to be calm, but this is the third time I've called. I have been waiting here for over an hour." The van finally arrived. When I went on board, I said to the driver, "You kept me waiting for over an hour." His response was, "Do you want a ride? Or don't you want a ride?" They provided the bare minimum of service: they did (finally) pick me up and take me to the service area. When I complained to the main office, I received what was clearly a canned apology. There was no acknowledgment that what happened to me was not their usual level of service. There was no offer of a discount or upgrade the next time I rented with them. Will I be renting with them again? No, never.

Reactive service is easy. It relies on generalized assumptions about what you think the customer needs and usually results in equally generic responses. The responses may solve a customer's current problem but rarely do they make customers feel like you care about them personally. At best it's a temporary solution to a bigger or growing problem. It's a bandage, not a cure.

A bottle of wine sent to your hotel room is lovely, but if it doesn't come with a note that addresses you by name (and spelled correctly), it doesn't have the same impact. What's efficient for your business may not make your customer feel like you care about them. Our office building doesn't have a receptionist or a doorman. When Amazon tried to deliver a package during the COVID-19 lockdown, there was no one there to receive it. I called and asked that it be redirected to my home. I was told there was no way to do that; they would try to deliver it three times and if they weren't successful the merchandise would be returned to Amazon and my account would be credited. I was frustrated, and shocked. Returns and restocking cost them money. Why don't they have a redirect procedure? (UPS has one, but it doesn't always work and it's easy to get lost in their system.)

## Play Where the Puck Is Going to Be

In the new world of customer service, we all need to be *proactive*. Proactive customer service means preemptively looking for every opportunity to find innovative ways to make them want to stay. Hockey legend Wayne Gretzky said, "A good hockey player plays where the puck is. A great hockey player plays where the puck is going to be."

*In business, good service gives the customer what they want. Great service gives the customer what they didn't know they wanted.* It's that proactive element of pleasurable surprise that catches their attention.

Proactive customer service is the gold standard. Your customer, whether they are aware of it or not, expects to be taken care of. Proactive service is the ability of your business to anticipate your customer's unanticipated needs and give them something they didn't even know they wanted or required.

We embrace this principle when we're planning a destination event. For example, if we're taking 125 guests to a resort or city they've never been to, we want them to have the best experience possible. We look for opportunities at every touch point to make guests feel special. I've always said that a well-informed guest is a happy guest.

We send a save-the-date notification with a link to a password-protected website that has all the information they need: where they're going, how to get there, the expected weather, a schedule of events, and the dress code for each event. There will be a list of optional activities and excursions and contact information for the event coordinator. When we receive an RSVP, we send a confirmation package to the guest. The package repeats the information from the website, and if it's necessary, contains reminders about passports and other travel information. We include personalized luggage tags for each guest. We ask all guests if they have any dietary restrictions or special needs and request their travel information so we can create a dossier for each person. This gives us the data we need to deliver a seamless and personalized experience for everyone attending the event.

Our travel concierge meets each guest at the airport. She carries a clipboard with the logo of the event (which is used on all the invitations, correspondence, and other items like menus and schedules) and the guests' names. At the hotel, there's a welcome note with reminders of all the events, their times, and dress codes for each one. We always like to leave each guest a welcome gift, like a local specialty snack, sunscreen, a fragrant candle, or a poem from the couple. For turndown service there's chocolate or a hangover remedy or another poem or meaningful quote to cap off a wonderful night and let the guest know their hosts are thinking of them, even when the event is over.

Proactive service is leveraging the power of the element of surprise—like the now iconic chocolate chip cookies that DoubleTree by Hilton gives customers at check-in. In the midst of the COVID-19 pandemic, DoubleTree released the recipe, scaled to the home kitchen. Not only did it give fans of the cookies a way to satisfy their craving while they couldn't stay at a DoubleTree, it reminded them that those cookies would be waiting for them (maybe individually packaged this time) at a DoubleTree hotel when they were able to travel again.

Proactive service is making a guest's experience feel fresh every time they're with you. For example, a friend brought her dog, Gina, on vacation to the same hotel several years in a row. Last year when she got to her room, she found a framed picture of her with her dog. One of the staff had found the image on her Instagram account and thought it would make her feel more welcome. Gestures like these are completely unexpected and create an immediate emotional connection.

Proactive customer service is personalized customer service delivered with extreme attention to detail. In chapter 2, I discussed how you get information on your client or customers. Now how do you use it? I produced a client's son's bar mitzvah and she recently returned to work with me on her son's wedding. I know she wants to meet at 5:30 p.m. so her son and his fiancée can be there and that she wants a half hour with me alone before the meeting. I know she likes white Burgundy, so I have a chilled bottle open when she arrives, and we can have a glass while we have a relaxed discussion. When her son and the bride-to-be arrive, their names are on the screen in the conference room and on a sheet with an agenda for the meeting.

Jack Ezon of Embark Beyond points out that where there is an overwhelming amount of information and too many choices, "curating" experiences for your targeted customer is a way to create personalized service. One of my favorite (and admittedly very high-end) examples is at the Rosewood Las Ventanas al Paraiso in Cabo San Lucas. Managed by the late, legendary hotelier Ed Steiner, no detail of a guest's stay was too small to command his attention. At a good hotel you may find a premade sewing kit among your amenities. Here the staff who clean the room takes note of the colors of your clothes and create a custom sewing kit for you. I had a similar (and again, admittedly high-end!) experience at the Four Seasons Hong Kong, where I hung a pink-lined suit and pink shirt in the closet and when I took them out to wear found that a pair of pink silk knot cuff links had been put in the sleeves. I travel with my own pillow, and when I returned to my room after a workout, found it encased in a pillowcase that matched the bed linens, embroidered with my initials.

During another stay at the Four Seasons in Hong Kong, I returned the beautiful basket of pastries placed on the table at breakfast untouched because I don't like to eat baked goods made with white flour in the morning. On day three of my stay, the basket on the table was filled with gluten-free breads and baked goods. I hadn't said anything about my preferences. I realized that not only was someone watching what went out of the kitchen, they were watching what came back in, and thinking about why. It's the same principle as those DoubleTree cookies that are baked fresh on-site every day. It makes you feel like they were baked just for you.

●

## Refinement Isn't What You Think It Is

I believe that proactive service includes a layer of refinement. That's all very well in your business, you might say, but that doesn't apply to *every* business. Yes, it does. When I talk about refinement, it's not about starched napkins and 800-thread-count sheets. It's about entering an environment—real or virtual—that makes you feel welcome and comfortable. For example, most women I know hate going into a store to buy a bathing suit. Why? The lights in the dressing room are horrible. They're harsh and emphasize every bump and wrinkle, even if you don't have bumps and wrinkles. Think how much more pleasant the experience could be for the customer if the lighting were more flattering. Think how much more money a customer might spend if she wasn't in such a hurry to get out of that dressing room.

Refinement isn't exclusive to private or expensive venues. Let's talk about refinement and public bathrooms. For me it's a measure of how much an establishment cares about their customers. There's a cancer center in Westchester where someone I know goes for treatment. Chemotherapy and radiation take a toll on one's appearance. The first time he used the men's room, he looked in the mirror and was surprised to see how good he looked: it was the lighting. A small detail, but one that made a big difference to my friend, and other patients there.

I've been to an event at a luxury hotel where they used cheap, harsh bulbs in the bathrooms. There was an overflowing waste container, no toilet paper in the stalls, and a dying plant in the corner. It was an unpleasant experience and colored my opinion of the hotel. On the other hand, at Bryant Park behind the main branch of the New York Public Library, the restrooms are decorated with crown molding and imported tiles. There's a full-time attendant, fresh flowers, and a soundtrack of classical music. I recently stopped at a gas station and had to use the bathroom. I approach gas station bathrooms the way I approach airplane bathrooms: only when absolutely necessary and with extreme caution. In this case I needn't have worried. The room was clean, the floor had been mopped, there was a small vase of flowers, and it smelled *fresh*. There was a sign on the door that showed the bathroom was cleaned every hour and signed by the person who did the cleaning. That's refinement, even at a rest stop by the side of a highway.

Refinement is in the details. Think about how you offer your customer a drink of water. Do you hand them a plastic bottle? Or a bottle and glass? If the setting is appropriate, what if you offered water in a real glass with ice and a choice of a lemon, lime, or orange slice? What if you presented it on a small tray? It takes a little more effort, not a lot more money, and it creates a big positive and elegant first impression.

●

## The 3x5s

No matter how elegant the place settings or how polite the server, even stellar service can be bad service if it's not delivered consistently. Without consistency, you have no credibility: good service one day and bad service the next is a fail. No matter how often you deliver stellar service, most people will focus on the one time you didn't, and that's the story they'll tell to their friends. If the same diner with a dairy allergy comes in and communication between reservations, the server, and kitchen breaks down at any point, that restaurant has not only potentially put the health of that diner at risk, but likely also lost a customer for good. If there's a breakdown between the waitstaff and the kitchen, someone could become seriously ill. That's what happened to a friend of my literary agent. She was clear with the server that she was highly allergic to all dairy products. The server assured her it would not be a problem, but in fact the nuts in her dish had been sauteed in butter. Even that small amount made her so sick she had to be rushed to the hospital. It turns out the server did tell the kitchen staff about the allergy and that no butter should be put into the dish but did not confirm that those instructions had been followed when he retrieved and served the dish.

Creating templates and protocols ensures every client gets a consistent experience. In my office, once my team hears the door buzzer ring, it's showtime! My team knows what to do. It doesn't matter whether they've been with the company one day or five years because we have books of reproducible protocols that everyone studies and can refer to. Consistency in service doesn't mean you can't personalize the experience. I have a template for how we set up our conference room for a business lunch, but the lunch menu isn't the same every time. If a client is vegetarian, or keeps kosher, or doesn't eat gluten, what we serve reflects that.

It's why I created the 3x5s, the five things that you do before, during, and after a customer engages with your service. Whenever there is a service module that you want to develop or create, there are three stages to the process:

1. Preproduction, or all the things you need to set up to deliver that service module.
2. Production, or what you do when that module is "live."

3.  Postproduction, or reset and reorder; the things
    you do to set yourself up to successfully reproduce
    that module the next time.

These types of protocols not only ensure a smooth customer experience, they also provide a framework for your employees to provide the gold standard of customer service with
confidence. Each customer interaction has a beginning, a
middle, and an end, but you may not need to have to have
three fives for your business. It could be the 3x3s, or the 3x4s
or the 3x2s.

When I worked with NetJets, a company that sells shares
of private business jets, I was charged with shifting the perception of the company to one that was associated with safety,
but not luxury, to one of safety *and* luxury. First we looked at
all the touch points of client interaction. NetJets clients lived
all over the world and 9:00 a.m. for a client in Hong Kong
might be 9:00 p.m. at the company headquarters. It didn't
matter what time of day a call came in, there needed to be a
real person to answer the call. They would pull up the digital
file for the owner and fill in the information for their flight.
Did they like a particular kind of plane? What time would
they prefer to leave? Did they want to snack, or did they prefer
a full catered meal? Did they want a specific wine, brand of
soda, or mineral water? Did they need ground transportation
on both sides of the flight? Once the arrangements were final-
ized, the client would get a confirmation.

Making the physical changes to the décor of the cabins and
to catering wasn't difficult, but changing the behavior of the
pilots was. I discovered that pilots are a little like doctors in
that they have your life in their hands, and they think that's
all they have to worry about. But like a doctor who needs to

work on his bedside manner, I had to work with the pilots to get them to understand that customer relations was also an essential part of their job. Too often a pilot would walk into the waiting room and yell, "Okay, who's going to Aspen?" Not a luxury experience.

Pilots use checklists in the process of getting ready to take off, in flight, and during landing, so implementing the 3x5s was a logical next step: five things each pilot was required to do before, during, and after the flight when they interacted with the customer. Every nuance of pilot-client interaction was addressed.

1.  We sent the pilot the names and pictures of their passengers via their cell phones, so they could discreetly check the images against the waiting passengers. When the pilot walked into the waiting room, they were in uniform; the top button of their jacket was fastened, they were wearing their hat, and they had their business card in hand. No dark glasses, no chewing gum. When they identified their client and approached them at ten feet, they smiled as they walked toward them.

2.  At five feet, the pilot put out their hand for a handshake. If the client didn't want to shake hands, the pilot put their hands behind their back, nodded, and bowed gently.

3.  The pilot introduced themselves: "Good morning, Mrs. Smith, my name is Captain Speed. I'm going to be flying you to Aspen today. Can I help you with your hand luggage? We need to make our way to the plane." If they had flown with the client before, the pilot reminded them: "You may not

remember this, but I flew you and your family for
Thanksgiving to Palm Beach earlier this year." This
created an emotional connection.

4.  Helped the client board the plane.
5.  Got them settled in their seat and any baggage
    properly stowed.

On the plane they were to:

1.  Go over safety standards and procedures.
2.  Let the client know the flight plan and flying time.
3.  Offer them something to drink and tell them about
    catering options.
4.  On arrival, help them off the plane.
5.  Walk them to the FBO (Field Base Operations).

To follow up, they:

1.  Made sure the client had all their luggage.
2.  Made sure the client got to their car or car service.
3.  Checked on the plane and noted any repairs that
    had to be made.
4.  Recorded any customer concerns or complaints
    and communicated all this to owner services.
5.  Communicated any issues with 3 and 4 to the
    main office.

## At Colin Cowie Lifestyle, the
## 3x5s Looks Like This

Preparation:

1. When we get an inquiry, we take down the (potential)
   client's basic information, including what kind of
   event and their budget, and make an appointment.
2. We do research on Google and social media. If we
   have mutual friends or acquaintances, I might put
   in a call. I want as much information as possible.
3. We decide which team members will be at
   the meeting and prepare a personalized slide
   presentation.
4. The day of the appointment we set up the
   conference room and cue the slide show, including
   a welcome slide with the client's name. There is a
   selection of drinks (alcoholic and nonalcoholic)
   and snacks (espresso beans, cheese, nuts, fruit).
   Espresso, coffee, or tea and both dairy and
   nondairy milk are available.
5. We prepare a gift bag with a handwritten note for
   the client to take home.

When the client arrives:

1. A team member is waiting downstairs to
   identify and greet the client and bring them
   to the office.
2. The client is seated in the conference room facing
   the glass wall so they can see the office activity and
   take in the elegance of the surroundings. They are

offered something to drink, a snack, and asked if they'd like to use the restroom.

3. We introduce the team, make our presentation, and explain how we work.

4. We gather as much information as we can about the client and what they're looking for. We answer any questions we can on the spot and make a note of others for follow-up.

5. When the meeting is over, we give the client an information folder and gift bag and thank them for their time. We walk them to the elevator and wait until the door closes before leaving.

Regroup and reset:

1. Clean the conference room.
2. Put away the food and do the dishes.
3. Have a follow-up meeting with the team to discuss how the meeting went.
4. Determine next steps: What needs to be done to close this deal?
5. Implement next steps.

At a hair salon you know from your files that Mrs. Patel doesn't like to wait, likes her coffee black with one brown sugar on the side, likes Maria to wash her hair, and always sees Felipe for a cut.

Part 1:

1. Greeting: "Hello, Mrs. Patel. It's nice to see you again. You're seeing Felipe for a cut today?"

2. Make her feel at home and cared for: "Maria will be
   washing your hair. She'll be with you in a minute.
   May I get you a coffee? Black with one brown sugar,
   correct?"

Part 2:

1. Hair wash and Felipe comes back to take Mrs. Patel
   to his station.
2. Haircut and any adjustments the client thinks are
   needed.

Part 3:

1. Greeting: "You look lovely as always, Mrs. Patel. Was
   everything to your satisfaction?"
2. Payment and follow-up: "Would you like to pay
   using the card we have on file? The usual 20
   percent tip for Felipe? Would you like to make
   another appointment? Would you like to book your
   color next time also?"

For the concept of the 3x5s (or 4s, or 3s, or 2s) to work, you
can't do the first and last part and forget the middle. They all
relate to each other and that's how you create the best customer experience. This is why proactive customer service depends on solid teamwork, gathering information, and clear
communication. At the salon, this could start with a pre-
opening staff meeting to look over the appointments of the
day and be prepared for each guest. If you have a team that
has flexible hours, as often happens at a salon or spa, you
could design a virtual or IRL check-in before each stylist

starts their appointments, and the same kind of debrief when they leave for the day.

Consistency has to be tempered with common sense, of course! Having information doesn't mean using it on autopilot. I know Mr. Smith enjoys scotch, and I'll offer that to him at a 5:00 p.m. meeting. If we're sitting down at 10:00 a.m., I might jokingly say, "I know you prefer scotch, but maybe not so early in the day? How would you like your coffee? Or would you prefer something else?"

Proactive service anticipates the changing commercial climate and responds to evolving customer needs. Take Uber. At first, shared ride customers had to figure out how to split the fare; now you can do it in the app (and Uber makes a little money every time you do so). In the beginning, you had to write an email to cancel a car; now you can do it with the click of a button on the app. Uber instituted "Quiet Mode," which allows riders to request a driver who won't talk to them. The company realized groups were ordering individual cars to be picked up at the same location, so they implemented Uber Events, so riders can order multiple cars to the same location at the same time. Uber raised the bar and exploited the many opportunities they uncovered. And once that bar is raised, you can be sure your competition is raising theirs. If you don't have what your customer has come to expect, they won't be buying what you have to offer.

●

### First Impressions Count

Where does your customer's experience begin? When they've crossed the threshold into your physical or cyber space, what kind of journey are you taking them on? Very often, the

person who is at the front desk or answers the phone or
email queries is the least-experienced and lowest-paid member of the team. I think that's a mistake. That person creates
the first impression of your company for your customer and
is the first line of communication between your client and
the rest of your team. If they're having a bad day, if they're
rude, cold, or dismissive, that colors your customer's entire
experience. Even if the rest of their interactions are positive,
the story they tell themselves and others will begin with that
negative impression.

I recently checked into a hotel and it was clear the young
man at the desk was so rude I had to speak up. I told him, "I'm
going to walk outside and give you another chance to welcome
me properly." I did and this time he welcomed me professionally and politely. Over the course of my stay, we spoke several
times. He apologized for our initial encounter; his girlfriend
had broken up with him the night before and he had allowed
his (understandably) bad mood to color his professional interactions, making me bear the brunt of what he was feeling.
If we hadn't had that conversation, regardless of how hard the
members of the hotel staff worked to make my stay a pleasant
one, my first impression of the service at the hotel would have
been a bad one. If no one else had brought his behavior to his
attention, it could have affected many other guests' first impressions of the brand. If your customer's first experience
with your service or product is a rude or unpleasant employee,
they may not give you another chance.

Teamwork means that every person in your organization
has an important role. Like the friend of my literary agent,
when a diner tells a member of a restaurant staff that they
cannot eat dairy, that information should be taken seriously
and communicated to the person's server. It's the server's responsibility to inform the kitchen that the walnuts in the

spinach salad cannot be fried in butter and to confirm in the kitchen that no butter was used before they serve the customer. Once the server advises the customer that there are no dairy products used in the salad, that person can relax and enjoy their meal.

I was consulting on a luxury real estate sales project. The first person from the organization that customers met was the valet/doorman. The person the company hired was—I'm being polite here—sloppy. His shirt and pants did not look clean and were not pressed. He did not open the car door, did not greet the clients, and answered questions in monosyllables. My first recommendation was to get a new doorman who would better represent the standards of the property, make a good impression. If she arrives in the rain, he should greet her with an umbrella, if she has a dog, a dog treat, or with a child, a teddy bear for the little one. He could also communicate valuable information to the sales team. How? By listening and transmitting that information to the team. I don't mean eavesdropping or leaning in to invade someone's privacy. I'm talking about being alert to what people are discussing in your presence. Perhaps the client spoke more frankly to her broker than to the sales agent. There's nothing wrong with a doorman asking how a departing client liked the building or the apartment they'd come to see. Did the customer mention that she liked the layout of the kitchen but not the finishes? Was she looking for bigger closets or en suite baths for all the bedrooms? Sales can use that information in their follow-up email or call to close the deal. They could offer to move a wall between a bedroom and the living room to give the buyer more living space, to let the buyer choose new countertops in the kitchen, or to create a custom closet in the master bedroom. Often the person who earns the least money can help close the biggest sale of the day.

Your customer-facing staff are also your early warning system. If Mrs. Patel is upset when she gets to the front desk for her hair appointment, the receptionist can put the rest of the staff on alert. If it comes time to pay the bill and she doesn't want to leave her usual tip, the receptionist can speak to the stylist and find out if there was an issue during the appointment. That gives the stylist or salon owner the opportunity to correct a misunderstanding or mistake and offer a way to fix a problem.

KEEP IN MIND:

- Proactive service is the gold standard. Reactive customer service corrects a situation when something goes wrong but doesn't anticipate or prevent a problem from happening.
- Play where the puck is going to be. Proactive service anticipates customers' needs and gives them what they didn't know they wanted.
- Implement the 3x5s. Proactive service requires templates and protocols to ensure every client gets a consistent experience.
- First impressions count. Your customers' first impression of your service or business colors their entire experience.

NOW ASK YOURSELF:

- Am I providing my customers with reactive or proactive service?
- What can I do to personalize my customers' experience?
- What kind of refinement can I bring to my customers' experience?
- How can I apply the concept of the 3x5s to my business?

# four

*Making an*
*Emotional*
*Connection*

C reating an authentic connection with your customer means making them feel like they're the focus of your attention. That's at the core of truly great customer service and at the heart of why people stay loyal to a brand, a store, or to a service provider. I believe today if your customer doesn't have an emotional connection to your product or service they will go somewhere else.

When you have an emotionally connected customer, they buy more of the products and services you're offering. When they're emotionally connected, they visit your website, store, or office more often. They show less price sensitivity. An emotionally connected customer pays more attention to your emails, texts, or physical mail. They are more open to your recommendations and suggestions, and they recommend you to their friends. They have twice the lifetime value of a satisfied regular customer. They are your best ambassadors, as they will talk about the great experience they enjoyed with your company.

## Seducing Your Customer

I know the word *seduction* has negative connotations, that it implies someone is getting you to do something you don't want to do, usually in a sexual way. But *seduce* also means to attract powerfully, and if you're going to get and keep your customer, that's what you have to do: attract powerfully. You do that by creating an emotional connection. An emotional connection means I've affected the way you feel in a positive way. Our interactions have surprised, delighted, or satisfied you. I've engaged your heart and mind. If I don't do it right—you're disappointed or dissatisfied—then I've failed and I haven't created that connection, and you'll move on.

I'm not talking about coming on to your client. It's got nothing to do with how tight my pants are or how many buttons are undone on my shirt. It means knowing who your client is, what they want, and knowing how to appeal to them. I'm talking about putting your best business foot forward to make yourself as attractive to your customer as possible. You want your client or customer to look at your product, service, website, office, or store and think, "This is the gold standard." Great customer service isn't enough to attract and keep your client; it only comes alive when you enhance that service with an emotional connection.

Making that connection starts with your attitude. It begins with respect for your client and for their time. Have you ever stood at a reception desk for what seems like forever while the receptionist was on the phone and didn't acknowledge you? I know I have. It's frustrating, to say the least. In some cases, as at a doctor's office, getting off the call quickly may not be possible; however, looking at you and nodding or making eye contact at least acknowledges that you're there. Your customer wants to feel seen and recognized in all their interactions, virtual and in real life, with you.

Always put your client on a pedestal to make them feel special. I've said this before and it bears repeating: It doesn't matter what your product or service is. If you don't have customers, you don't have a business. I remind myself every day that I'm here because of my clients. And so are you. Sometimes people forget this.

It's easy to sit back when you're busy and have all the work you need or want. There was a time when I had so much business that I used to handpick who I wanted to work with. I regret that, because I could have developed any number of repeat clients from the events I turned down. I'd love to turn back the clock because today I've never worked harder not only to get the client but to keep the client. The landscape has changed so much and I and my team value every single phone call that comes in. We're keenly aware that we're in a highly competitive environment; from the time we get that first email inquiry or call, we treat each potential client like gold and provide the gold standard in customer service.

If there's a phone message or email query, we set up a firm date and time for a call so we can avoid a phone tag situation. Our job on that first call is to make an emotional connection with the client. The initial questions our team asks aren't just about gathering information—Where are you calling from? When is the wedding? How many guests?—they're also an opportunity to find common ground that we can use to nurture that connection.

For example, a potential client tells one of my team that they want to do a destination beach wedding next spring for their daughter. "Have you thought about Bermuda? It's one of my favorite places, and the weather is beautiful in the spring." "I can't believe you suggested that! How did you know? Bermuda is the first place on our wish list!" There's your opportunity for an emotional connection. Or take the online pet supply company Chewy. They know many of their customers consider their pets their family, their "fur babies." When you sign up for an account, you fill out not just your information but your pet's as well. When you talk to customer service, one of the first things they ask is your pet's name and birthday. The call becomes about your pet and *their* preferences; there's your emotional connection. Tailored Pet creates personalized recipes for your dog and delivers them to your door. There's a label on the food with your dog's name, their age, size, activity level, sensitivities, and wellness goals, as well as the ingredients. If your pet doesn't like it, they'll work with you until they find a formula that appeals to them, or you get your money back. The Farmer's Dog, the dog version of farm to bowl, provides the same kind of service.

## What's Your Brand's Story?

Stories are powerful connectors. Having a clear vision of what you and your organization stand for and making sure that vision is infused in every touch point with your consumer enables you to tell your story and create the appropriate emotional connection. My business showcases lifestyle, luxury, and exceptional service. It's what my clients come to me for. That's what the physical space of our lobby and office, our websites, our stationery, and even our business cards are designed to reflect. While I didn't design every aspect of those things, I was deeply involved in making the choices of how my company and I would be represented. It was important to me because I see these touch points as opportunities to reinforce our brand and create strong connections with our clients. If I were an accountant, the cardstock of my thank-you notes would probably be less important (depending on my clientele), and I'd want my website to convey efficiency and trustworthiness.

When I'm creating an event, I'm always guided by what I call my clients' DNA—what makes them and their story unique. Whether it is a corporation, a product, a service, there is always something that sets them apart. What does your physical or cyber space say about your business?

You have a limited window of time to engage with your customer and make that connection, so when your customer looks at your website, physical space, or product they should think, "I'm in the right place. This is just what I was looking for." You want your client or customer to feel that you care about them and their needs. You want them to feel embraced and welcomed. In our office, the slide show we put up for prospective clients reflects what we know about them and what we think they'll relate to. Say I'm meeting with a new client. She's forty and a successful entrepreneur. She's told me her favorite color is hot pink and her favorite flowers are peonies. It will be a small gathering of fifty to seventy-five people, and she wants a country setting not too far from New York City. Now, I know she's a busy woman, and we'll want to keep the meeting to forty-five minutes or an hour at most. If it's possible, I'll make sure we have a flower arrangement with pink peonies in the conference room; if peonies aren't available, the arrangement will use other pink flowers. The events I'll showcase in the slide show will feature countryside venues and not the five-hundred-person extravaganzas.

•

## Make It Personal

I know I'm in a rarified category when it comes to the deeply personal customer service I provide. However, even a small business can create an emotional connection in the simplest way. Have you ever been at a bakery counter and seen the salesperson give a child a cookie? It's lovely to see that child's face light up, and that gesture also made the parent who's spending the money feel good. Here's a secret: don't be afraid to use humor or get personal. If you can make someone smile or laugh, you've made a strong emotional connection.

You have information about your customers or clients. Use it! When I go to my gym and scan my card, the person at the desk greets me by name. "I see you took a Pilates class last week; there's one tomorrow—should I sign you up?" They're creative and look for opportunities to engage with me—and all of their customers—directly every time. The other day they had a number of trainers on-site who weren't busy, so they set out two stretching tables, and offered a free stretch after your workout. Brilliant. Not only was I grateful for the treat, it made me feel wonderful physically, and I wound up booking (and paying for) additional sessions.

I recently attended a conference held at the uber-fabulous Amanyara resort in Turks and Caicos. One of the sales executives sent a bottle of Rare Champagne to welcome me, along with a note that read:

*Happy 222 [+1] days of your love story since 02/22/20.*
*May your days and nights be wrapped in romance.*
*Time to celebrate.*

I had been married on February 22, 2020. It blew me away that she had taken the time to count how many days it had been since the wedding and include the number in our card with reference to 2/22.

Engaging your customer or client emotionally doesn't require a face-to-face meeting. It does require a personal connection, and that's possible even in a large-scale business. Chewy shines here again. I know someone who called the company to return unopened pet food when his dog died. The first thing the representative did was to offer her condolences. She told the man they would refund the money, and he could donate the food to his local shelter. The company also sent a small floral arrangement with a condolence note. The company connected with their customer on multiple levels: caring, compassion, understanding, and service.

Yes, there is information that you can get via an automated response, but if you give people the opportunity to speak to a live human being without having to go through yet another menu, you automatically go to the top of the queue in their opinion. It may not be that convenient for you to put "speak to a representative" as a first choice on a menu, but it makes your customer feel like you value them and understand that their time is valuable too. By the time I get to the second automated menu, I just hang up. Unless, of course, I'm dealing with the IRS or the cable company.

This is another place where I think Apple excels, even though talking with a person, or an in-person visit to a Genius Bar, is the last option they give you. If you have a problem with an Apple device, their triage system, which starts on their website, is simple and intuitive. You give them the serial number of your device. Can't find it? They'll show you exactly where on your device to look. If you want to chat online you get an almost immediate response from a real person, not a bot. If you want to speak to a tech, you leave your phone number and you get a message that you'll receive a call back in four minutes. Then your phone actually rings within four minutes! While you're waiting for the tech to connect, they ask what kind of music you want to listen to until they get on the line and offer five options. You get connected and the tech will stay on the phone as long as it takes to solve your issue. If you're upset or frustrated, they don't try to tell you not to be. They're empathetic. If they can't solve the problem, they'll set up an appointment at a Genius Bar for you. When you get off the phone, they send a follow-up survey. They want to know not just that the tech was able to fix your problem, but that you felt the person on the other end of the line *cared* about your problem.

Speaking of phones, if your client is calling your company, what's their experience? We've all been kept on hold for five, fifteen, thirty minutes while a recorded message tells us "Your call is important to us." If you're keeping me on hold for thirty minutes, I don't have the impression I'm that important to you. In a world of cell phones, international connections, and dropped calls, the first thing a customer-facing team member should ask a client is, "What is your phone number?" so they can call back if the call is disconnected. If they can, they should also give the customer *their* number. It's less of an issue in our business—and certainly not in my office—but how many times have you been on hold for forty minutes and just as your call is about to be picked up, you're cut off? I've lost count, especially when I'm dealing with travel arrangements. Sometimes a long wait is unavoidable, but there are ways to avoid frustrating or

angering your customers. For example, a friend needed a re-
placement turntable to her microwave and called a parts broker. While the wait to speak to a representative wound up being
forty-five minutes, the call management software told her
where she was in the queue and updated the message as her
position changed. She put the phone on speaker and was able
to work while she waited. Verizon and many other companies
now give you the option to leave your number for a callback.
You keep your place in the call queue and they do call you
back. It's a brilliant solution to an annoying problem.

Making an emotional connection with your client also means
making sales transactions as easy as possible, especially online. That means not having to open multiple pages and filling
out the minimum number of fields. It means only having to
give your information once, and if you need assistance, not
having to repeat it for each tier of help . It means having a real
person available if there's a problem and empowering that
person to do what is necessary—within reason—to close the
sale, whether on the phone or via live chat. A woman I know
tried to buy a piece of jewelry on a website. When it came
time to check out, the space for the credit card security number only permitted her to enter three numbers. Her credit
card used a four-digit code. Unable to complete the transaction, she tried to call but couldn't get through. She went to
online chat. The representative told her that no one else with
her kind of card had reported the same issue (essentially
blaming her for the problem and invalidating her experience)
and let her know she was going to ask another person for
assistance with the web page. After waiting thirty minutes, the
customer closed the page and walked away from the transaction. Why couldn't the representative have taken the information herself, or connected her with the order department and
allowed the customer to place the order over the phone?

The same thing goes for return policies, especially in the age of online shopping. If it's not easy and painless, your customer won't be buying from you again. Here again, Amazon sets the bar. You fill out your reason for the return online and receive a Q scan. You take the package to UPS or arrange to have them pick up the package. The UPS employee scans the code and prints the return label and takes care of the return. Simple and easy.

Sometimes making an emotional connection with a client depends on who's actually connecting with the customer. If I'm meeting with a young bride and groom-to-be, I'll make sure that I include younger members of my team as well. It may be my name on the door, but I know a younger client wants to feel like they can talk to someone with a shared language and experience. It's the reason (and I talk about this in chapter 9) why your customer-facing team members are so important. I think it's so important to select the right people to fulfill the obligations of the role. The emotional connection to your service or product starts with whoever answers the phone, emails, or even who answers the door.

●

## Keeping the Connection

Once you're connected, how do you keep that connection going? Communication. Your customer wants to feel valued and appreciated, but communicating with them can be an exercise in walking the fine line between too much and just enough. You have so many tools at your disposal: email, texts, Instagram, Twitter, and messaging apps like WhatsApp.

We were hired by our Hong Kong client on the basis of our phone conversations; we had never met face-to-face. My producers took a scouting trip to Sydney to explore event venues, which we were planning to share with the client with an online presentation. While in Sydney, the producers realized that they could fly back to the US via Hong Kong. They arranged to meet with the client in person and rerouted their tickets. That meeting was the foundation for a decade-long relationship with our client's family.

What can you do to engage the next step? You can't sit back and think "I'm done." The battle is not over. When a potential client leaves our office after the first meeting, we wait to hear from them. If we haven't heard back in twenty-four hours, I or one of the team will follow up with an email, telling them how much we enjoyed meeting them and asking if we can answer any questions. Would they be interested in scheduling another meeting?

If they don't respond, we'll wait another day and email again. If they've given us their cell phone number, we'll send a text. Often we get a message apologizing for not getting back to us sooner. Sometimes they make another appointment, sometimes they say they're still thinking, sometimes we get the "We've decided to go in another direction, but we look forward to working with you on future events." (I know they're just being polite, but I hate those emails. It's a dishonest, automated response. I'd rather someone tell me *why* they didn't choose me. It might give me useful information!)

I was determined to work on a highly sought-after celebrity wedding that was taking place on the West Coast. I had a wonderful video call with the bride and felt very confident that we would be working together, but she decided to work with someone local. She felt she wanted someone who could be there every step of the way. I called and asked if she would meet with me in person. When she agreed, I flew out and spent the day with the bride. We bonded over our shared vision for her wedding, and I promised I would always be as accessible to her as I was on that day. I flew back to New York the same evening and got the call the next day that we would work together. I was as good as my word: we set up weekly Skype calls so we could speak face-to-face, and of course we used texts, emails, and phone calls as well. Going the extra mile (in this case three thousand extra miles) and making the emotional connection not only gave me the opportunity to create the wedding of her dreams, but also other events for her and her family in years to come.

If there's still no response, I may ask another member of the team to reach out. There have been times when my email went into spam or junk mail and another person's didn't. We thought we'd lost a deal when the door was still wide open.

Gracefully accepting *no* for an answer is also showing respect for your customer. However, often just a little more time and effort will close the deal. I'll call until I get a definite "No, we've decided to go with someone else." Persistence pays off, and your gut will tell you when it's time to retreat.

•

## Nurture Long-Term Relationships

I want to stay on my clients' radar, even when we're not doing business. During the COVID-19 quarantine, we had very little interaction with our clients. We sent notes to tell them we were thinking about them and to let them know how important they were to us. Some clients received a picture from their event. Others received jigsaw puzzles of a memorable scene from their party or event. Some got a set of glass coasters with eight amazing images from their last event. Some received formal Colin Cowie–designed face masks that would help them feel safe and stylish at the same time. We shared custom playlists with a note that said: "We hope this music fills your house with joy and keeps you going during these tough quarantine weeks." They were simple but effective ways at a variety of price points to maintain an emotional connection, and to keep us top-of-mind.

You have to be able to take the temperature of your client and take your cues from them; it's not just one-size-fits-all. This is where using your emotional intelligence comes into play. Some people want you to deal with them directly; others may want you to go through an assistant. You may not want to, but if that's the way they want to be communicated with, that's the way they want to be communicated with. You may have to copy four people on all emails or use a group text. Your client dictates.

The same rules apply if you're a company selling a product to a bigger audience. Your individual customer gets to tell you what kind of communication they want and how often they want to hear from you. I recently unsubscribed from a company's emails. When I did, I was directed to a page that asked why. One of the several reasons listed was: "I get too many emails from you." In fact, I did, but shouldn't they have asked me how often I wanted to hear from them when I signed up? Why did they *assume* that I would want to hear from them every day? Making assumptions about your clients or customers means you're not really doing the work of getting to know who they are, what they want, and what's important to them.

I ask my clients how they prefer to hear from me, and how often, and we come up with a plan. You can do the same. Everyone is different. The other day, a new client called to discuss an event. When I had the information he needed, I asked if I should call him. He preferred text. In some Asian and Middle Eastern countries, my clients like to use WhatsApp. In fact, I've planned an entire wedding, including floor plans and contracts, using WhatsApp rather than email or phone.

The language you use with your clients shows how much you understand and respect your clients or customers. Getting their name right is emotional connection 101—you might be surprised at how often people don't bother to learn to pronounce a name correctly or double-check the spelling on a client's name.

I was raised to always err on the side of formality until the other person tells me otherwise. I realize that this goes against the popular tide of informality, but the first time I'm in touch with someone I always start with Mr., Mrs., Ms., or Dr., in person or via email. If they tell me, "Please call me Margo," or "Please call me David," only then will I use their first name. That works in my business. For example, when I'm staying at a hotel and call downstairs for something, I say, "Good morning, it's Mr. Cowie." I don't say, "Hi, it's Colin here in 506." I'm speaking their language. You know the language of your customers, and what they prefer.

How else can you show you appreciate your customer? What about an unexpected gift or bonus? A lagniappe, as they say in New Orleans—a little something to remember you by. It's like the chocolate or a poem on your pillow at a hotel, or the thirteenth bagel you get when you buy a dozen. When a potential client leaves my office, they take a signed copy of one of my books and a handwritten note on my personal stationary. If I'm working on the event personally, there's a card with my cell phone number. Catbird, a jewelry company based in Brooklyn, sends notecards and matches (they also sell delicious candles and incense) with each mail order. Haus, an artisanal aperitif company based in Los Angeles, sends a personal Christmas card from the owner and their family.

A friend and her husband were traveling with another couple to Paris to celebrate two spouses' shared milestone birthdays. At the airport for their trip home, the two couples were sitting at the gate waiting to board the plane; they were flying economy. They started chatting with one of the first-class stewards. When he learned about the reason for the trip, he left and returned with four first-class amenity kits. It was such a lovely and unexpected gesture, and my friend still uses the kit (she's obviously replaced the products!) whenever she flies. Because of that one steward's sweet gesture more than twenty years ago and the connection it cemented, she still flies that airline whenever possible.

I see Christmas, birthdays, holidays, and, in my business, wedding anniversaries as good opportunities to reignite and sustain an emotional connection. Just showing up counts. Our corporate gifts are sourced from charities that Colin Cowie Lifestyle supports. I always send Christmas and birthday cards to our clients past and present, and to our creative partners. On a couple's first anniversary, they get a card. For some very special clients, I've had a duplicate of the top of their wedding cake made and sent that as a gift. I've also celebrated each anniversary thereafter with gifts that fit the particular year's theme: a book with their initials engraved on the cover for paper, a tray inscribed with lyrics from their first dance for leather, a replica of their reception centerpiece for flowers. These are things they will talk about with their friends and families, and those people may become my new clients.

Around my birthday, I get emails and mailers from many of the companies I buy from. *Ten percent off! Fifteen percent off!* Well, thank you, but a) everyone does this, so it's not really going to get my attention, b) I may not need what you're selling within the time limit of the offer, and there's always a time limit, and c) it's not really a gift. Unless I need something from you *right now*, there's a good chance I'll be able to get what I want for 20 percent off or more next time you have a sale. If you're offering a discount, why not send a sample or samples of your product as well? Sephora, for example, offers a birthday gift of samples that changes every month. I don't know anyone who goes into their store or on their website to pick up their gift and doesn't buy something else. Kiehl's offers generous samples of up to three different products when you buy either online or in one of their stores. When I fly JetBlue they always have a different lip balm or hand cream in the amenity bag. I've often gone out and purchased the regular size of one of the samples, and I think about where I found my favorite product. Offering a taste of what you have to offer is an opportunity to create an emotional connection and can often lead to a more substantial sale.

What I like about sending a card or a gift, even a token, is that my client or customer doesn't have to do anything. Often, we have our own photographer at an event, and we'll send our client a framed photograph that we've had taken. At a wedding, we might take a photograph of the parents and send it to the bride and groom. If we know there are some guests who might be potential clients at an event, I'll have the photographer take a great photograph of them and send it on. One of our clients mentioned that they liked a cookbook from a chef we proposed that they use for a wedding. We bought the cookbook, had the chef sign it, and sent it to them. These things are a surprise. They're unexpected. They're something people didn't know about, let alone they want, but they're happy when they think about it—and that makes them think of you.

Aligning yourself with what your customer cares about gives you two levels on which you can connect with them. First, you have a product or service that they want. Second, you are socially responsible and support a cause or charity that is meaningful to them. It makes people feel good to know that by buying something they want or need, they are giving someone something *they* need for free. Customers choose brands like Warby Parker, Toms, or Bombas not just because they have a well-designed, reasonably priced product (Warby Parker glasses, Toms shoes, Bombas socks) but because of their buy-one, give-one program. Making programs like this part of their corporate identity helps establish brand purpose, create brand recognition, and reinforce brand loyalty. It's part of their advertising and marketing so that part of their mission is always in front of their clients.

If buy one, give one doesn't work as a business model for you, what else can you do?

A restaurant could organize a food drive or take a portion of each meal check and donate it to a food pantry or other social cause.

A salon could offer free hair, makeup, or nail services to at-risk teens during prom season.

A stationery store could donate backpacks and school supplies to kids whose families can't afford them.

Send an email or get local (or national if you're big enough) media to let people know. Get the word out on social media. People feel good when they see that their purchases are doing good.

Before making a purchase or transaction, many buyers will check to see what kind of carbon footprint or social action commitment a company has. They ask themselves, "If I buy this product, am I supporting a politician with whom I disagree? Am I helping to exploit a vulnerable population? Does my purchase hurt the environment?"

Forging an emotional connection with your customer means going above and beyond the regular and expected. In today's market, regular will fall by the wayside. Connect the dots, look for the opportunities, and make the connection.

KEEP IN MIND:

- Seduce your customer by creating an emotional connection. An emotionally connected customer will buy more of what you're selling and is less price sensitive.
- An emotionally connected customer is your best brand ambassador.
- Your customer dictates what and when they want to hear from you.
- Keep the connection going. Look for unexpected opportunities to connect with your customer.
- Nurture long-term relationships. Even the smallest gesture can create a strong connection.

NOW ASK YOURSELF:

- What am I doing to create an emotional connection with my customers?
- How can I use an unexpected gift or token to create an emotional connection with my customers?
- Am I letting my customers know that I care about what they care about?

# five

*Every Complaint*

*Is an Opportunity*

Y ou only have one reputation, and it is priceless. How you deal with errors and complaints can increase or decrease its value. You have to protect that reputation at all costs: one blemish and it is no longer flawless. Even if a complaint isn't valid, you have to treat it as such.

In today's world people are able to voice their complaints on social media without a filter. I prefer to offer praise where I can because it always ensures good service when I return, but whenever I get bad service or there's a problem, I'm the first one to complain. I'm as specific as I can be about what went wrong. Ideally, I will go directly to someone who can address the issue right away or to a place on the website where I know I can get a response. The reason I believe in complaining is because when we don't complain — politely and constructively — the product or service provider can't fix what they don't know is broken. A lack of constructive criticism and feedback from clients or customers creates an environment of complacency.

When I'm looking for a product or service, I almost always look at the ratings and read consumer comments and reviews. Don't you? But when I'm reading them, I have to ask myself: What is the customer complaining or raving about, and why? If I'm looking at a restaurant, I want to know about the quality of the food and the service. Someone else may be looking at value for their money so they want to know about portion size in relation to price.

A complaint or compliment is data, and data is how you improve your customer's experience going forward. What can you get from that data? Do you dismiss it out of hand? Or is there something that you can do better? Is there something you should be doing more of? Or less?

You have to look at each complaint and decide whether you can do something about it, if it will influence your core customer, and what, if anything, you can do to address the issue. I wrote a book on big fabulous weddings, which was heavily illustrated and more expensive than your basic novel. It had straight five star reviews on an eBook store until one person decided that they would give me one star because they didn't approve of other people spending a lot of money on their weddings. There was also a customer who received a damaged book and gave it one star. Neither of these reviews were real reflections on the quality or the content of the book. There was nothing I could say to the woman who disapproved of lavish weddings; however, I did contact my publisher and asked that they look into the shipping issue.

What about the customer who complains about price?

Eileen Fisher makes simple, timeless, high-quality women's clothing. I've heard complaints that "it's very expensive for what it is," but Fisher's clothing is the opposite of disposable fast fashion. She's transparent about her sourcing, is committed to fair trade practices and sustainability, pays her employees and suppliers fairly, and explains how that translates to higher prices for her product. The customer who knows about the Fisher philosophy may complain about the sizing or a raveled seam, but not the price of the clothes.

If you're a restaurateur and a review says that $32 was too much for an entrée, can you drill down to see why they felt they had paid too much? Did they feel the portion size was too small? Was it not cooked to their liking? Did the menu description not align with the dish the customer was served? Were they comparing the experience at your restaurant to another that offered the same kind of food at a lower price point? If it's the only review out of twenty that complained about price, should you take that into account? If you can pinpoint why the customer gave you a negative review, you can decide whether it's something you need to address (a poorly prepared dish) or something you don't feel you need to (lowering the quality of your ingredients so you can charge less per serving).

When I'm looking at reviews, am I seeing the same kind of complaint in the reviews over and over, and over a long period of time? If that's the case, it tells me that the company or individual isn't using their customers' feedback to improve their product or service. If 30 percent of a restaurateur's customers are telling them that they had to wait twenty minutes before they saw a waiter, why aren't they addressing the problem? If I'm thinking of buying shampoo online, and I'm consistently seeing reviews that say the products are arriving damaged, there's obviously a problem in the shipping department that hasn't been dealt with.

•

## People Complain for a Reason

Let's acknowledge that while most people inherently are reasonable, there are a lot of mean, angry people out there and the internet gives them an unfiltered forum to be as vitriolic as they can. And yes, there are customers who will always find something that displeases them. We all deal with unreasonable people and their complaints. Unreasonable people have big mouths. Unreasonable people complain. They tell everyone who will listen to them how bad their experience was, how badly made the couch is, how unresponsive the salesperson was. You always need to take into account from whence a criticism cometh, but we're all in the business of customer service, and they're customers too.

When a customer complains, they're upset. Their expectations haven't been met, they're disappointed, and they feel like they've been let down. They want to know that you hear what they have to say and what *you're* going to do about it. I know that when something does go wrong—a client's flight is canceled or their plane has turned around, the shirt that they ordered didn't come in or it didn't fit properly—it's not always your fault. That's not the issue. It's your responsibility to do something about it. A lawyer once said to me, "Everybody has a story." Let your client tell theirs.

You have everything to lose and nothing to gain by ignoring a complaint. I've never been in a situation in my life where I've had a volatile person in front of me and I wasn't able to calm them down by saying I'm sorry and accepting responsibility. There's power in the immediate apology. Even in those situations where I'm only partially at fault, or not at fault at all, simply accepting responsibility can diffuse the situation, and gives me time to fix things. Sometimes simply listening and acknowledging their complaint is sufficient.

If they tell you that all of their guests at their event said their food was cold, you can tell them you'll speak to the caterer. Now, what resolution would make you happy? Some people might ask for the entire cost of the meal to be taken off the bill. Here I want to stop and say: accepting responsibility and paying for your mistake is not the same as being punished for your mistake. Comping one unhappy diner at a restaurant is not the same as refunding the cost of a hundred meals. There's nothing wrong with negotiating in this situation. There's always a middle ground between what they want and what you want. You might counter with the suggestion that you'll charge the meal at cost and take off your profit.

A mistake is not a disaster. You almost always have the opportunity to turn a mistake around. You really do. I look at a complaint as an opportunity to turn an unhappy customer into a loyal customer. A friend had a primary care doctor that she loved, but the billing department associated with the doctor's office was a nightmare. Because of their procedures, she wasn't being reimbursed and the billing office wasn't dealing with the problem. She wrote a letter to her doctor outlining the issues in detail and told her that as wonderful a physician as she was, and as sad as it would make her to leave, if the problems with accounting couldn't be fixed she would find another doctor. The day her doctor received the letter, she called my friend and apologized. She told her the situation was unacceptable and it was not the way her office should be run. She told my friend she had spoken to the head of the billing department and that he would personally rectify the situation. She gave my friend his direct line so she could call him if the problem continued. It didn't, and my friend still goes to that doctor a decade later.

You *want* to hear from a client if there's a problem. A silent, passive-aggressive customer can be a deadly customer; if they're not talking to you, they're probably complaining to someone else. A client was once gifted a day at a well-known salon. The day included a haircut, but she was happy with her current cut and declined. The stylist noted she had a lot of gray hair and suggested a semi-permanent rinse that would match her natural color and wash out in six to eight shampoos. It would be an extra charge as it wasn't included in the package price. My client agreed, so the stylist mixed and applied the color. When it was time to rinse the client's hair, she heard the stylist say, "Oh." *Not* what she wanted to hear. When she looked in the mirror, her naturally medium brown hair was now raven's-wing black. It was, we'll say, striking. The stylist offered to try and lighten the color, but the last thing my client wanted was to let this woman touch her hair again. The stylist assured her again it would wash out gradually.

If I had been that stylist, I would have comped her the color service. At least I would have offered her *something* — to come back for a free shampoo and blowout or a gift certificate for products. The stylist did nothing. She never said she was sorry. She never called my client to follow up. That's another thing: don't remain silent. It's better to stay in touch with someone until you know they're back in your court. You might not win them over, but at least you know you tried to rectify the situation.

And the color? It didn't wash out after six shampoos. It hadn't washed out after three months. Maybe the stylist mixed the formula incorrectly. Maybe she used dye instead of a rinse. That doesn't really matter. Has my client ever gone back to that salon? No. Has she told that story over and over? Yes.

●

## We All Make Mistakes

Acknowledging a problem and apologizing *immediately* is essential, but fixing something as soon as you can, rather than right away, is sometimes the best course of action. There's always a solution, even if it may not be obvious. When members of my team or I discover we made a mistake, we:

- **Acknowledge.** Don't be defensive. People want to be heard: listen to what your customer has to say and don't interrupt.
- **Apologize.** Reflect the customer's complaint in your response: "I'm sorry that your flight was canceled/ your package didn't arrive on time/the dress was too short."
- **Assess.** Get as much information about the situation or problem as you can. How serious is the problem? What needs to be done? How is your client feeling?
- **Assume Responsibility.** Assure your client that you'll deal with the problem.
- **Diffuse.** What can you do to make things right?
- **Recover and Reset.** Identify what went wrong and generate a checklist or procedure to prevent the same kind of mistake from happening again.

Here's an example. I was producing a wedding, and the bride insisted on a certain paper in a specific color ink for the invitations. We had a sample made and it looked wonderful. We signed off on everything. The invitations went out to more than 250 guests. For some reason, the foil ink on the outer envelope didn't adhere properly to the cardstock and rubbed off when it was handled by the postal service. More than half of the guests did not receive their invitations. When we realized what had happened, the bride—understandably—was *very* upset, and she let us know it. Here was the first thing we had set in motion on her wedding journey and there was a problem. She wondered if this was the way things were going to be as the wedding went forward. It was a dangerous situation for us to be in.

The first thing I did, of course, was to acknowledge that we had screwed up and apologize. (I've also had clients who complained that three people didn't receive invitations. It often turns out they gave us the wrong address, or zip code. I still apologize profusely and resend the invitations. We'll use FedEx or overnight mail if necessary.) I assured the bride that we would handle the situation without any additional cost to her. We immediately sent out beautiful electronic invitations to everyone, at our expense. I told the bride we would discount the price of the printed menus and place cards, and her thank-you cards would be a gift from me. The bride accepted our apology and appreciated my conciliatory gestures. The rest of her spectacular wedding went off without a hitch, and we stayed on good terms.

What did we do going forward? Since that event, every single invitation we send out is enclosed in a thin, clear envelope with the stamp on the outside and we've never had a similar problem. That's the whole idea of recovery: To make a good situation of a bad situation. To learn from our experiences so we know how to prevent it from happening again.

This happened thirty-five years into my career. No matter how good you are at what you do or how accomplished, mistakes will be made and things not in your control will go wrong. I'm big enough to say I'm sorry, and I believe you are too. It's true they're sometimes the most difficult words to say, but say them and mean it—not, "I'm sorry you're upset."

The next thing I want to do is get to the bottom of what went wrong. Here, timing is of the essence because the longer you take to respond the more ammunition for anger they have, and the more they'll need to vent before you can have a constructive exchange. You can always buy yourself a little time by saying, "Let me look into this and I'll get back to you." Then do it. If you say you'll get back to them in twenty minutes, set your alarm and get back to them in twenty minutes, even if it's only to say that you're still working on resolving the situation. Repeat as necessary.

## The Sincere Apology

The bigger the error, the more you need to apologize, even if you're apologizing for an error that someone else made. For minor snafus, like a late flower delivery, a phone call or even a text offering your sincerest apologies and assurances it will never happen again should suffice. Sometimes you just have to grovel. Even if your customer walks away, you don't want them to be able to say that you didn't apologize.

I was working on a charity event and the client promised that a sponsor's product would be prominently displayed at the entrance of the event and that the sponsor would be seated at a particular table. The client never told me or my team any of this, so the sponsor arrived and saw that none of what they had been promised was in place. There was no good solution to either of these issues. I could relocate the product, but it was too late for a new placement to have an impact on the assembled guests. I could have changed the seating arrangements but that would have meant displacing and upsetting other important donors. The sponsor made their displeasure very clear to the client, who in turn got very angry with me. It didn't matter that I hadn't been given the information I had needed; I still did my best to make amends. I emailed an apology and said I would look into what happened. I sent a follow-up explaining there had been a problem with communication and apologized again. I sent flowers with a handwritten note apologizing. I called. I texted. The client never responded. I had to walk away, but not until I had done everything I knew how to say I was sorry.

## Show Them You Care

The customer may not always be right, but you can almost never be too generous — within reason — when making amends. It's better to take a short-term monetary loss than have an unhappy customer. My IT manager was at Starbucks and tried to use the pad charger on a table. It didn't work. Later he emailed their customer service and let them know about the issue. They apologized for the inconvenience and sent him a five-dollar gift card. It was a small but appreciated gift for the customer that had a big impact. Not only did he keep going back to Starbucks when he had other options, but he told everyone in our office about it.

There is, in fact, a kind of science of sorry. Working with Uber, economist John List found that when customers got a simple apology for bad service, it didn't have much effect. But when the company offered upset customers a five-dollar coupon, customers remained loyal; they wanted to see the company take a loss, even if it was small one, to make up for their bad experience. List also found that "sorry" only worked once.

If there was a second or third bad experience, an apology, even accompanied by a coupon, was no longer effective.

At the Ritz-Carlton, every member of the staff was empowered to spend a certain amount of money if they could satisfy an unhappy customer or correct a problem on the spot. That is genius because, at the end of the day, addressing a complaint immediately, whether it's comping a dessert because an entrée wasn't to a guest's liking, offering an upgraded room, or refunding money, makes your customer feel like you not just listened, but *heard* them, and cared about their satisfaction.

There's a very expensive, very exclusive restaurant in New York's Hell's Kitchen where getting a reservation is almost impossible. It's one of those places where they turn up the music after 9:00 p.m. and everyone starts dancing whether they've eaten or not. The first time I went as a guest of a friend. I was very excited to taste the food. We no sooner got our food than the very loud music and the dancing started. So much for dinner. The next time I went, I was the host. I sent a letter to the manager explaining how the last time I was at the restaurant we spent a great deal of money and though the drinks were great, and we had a wonderful time dancing, we never got to eat. It was fun, but I'd heard so much about the food, and tonight I wanted to eat.

My guests and I arrived at the restaurant, and the first course came out in a timely way. Then nothing. Forty-five minutes went by, they cranked up the music, and then the rest of our dinner arrived. By that time, we didn't want to eat. I wrote to the manager again the next morning, telling them that this was the second time I'd come to the restaurant and had the same problem. She wrote a heartfelt note, telling me that the waiter assigned to our table forgot to put the rest of our order into the computer. She hoped I would come back and try them a third time.

What the manager didn't say was please come back as my guest, or your first martini's on me, or next time dessert is on the house. That's what she should have done. Will I go back? Never again. They screwed up on two occasions, I gave them the opportunity to fix it, and they didn't. Fewer and fewer people are willing to put up with being treated badly, and they're unwilling to risk repeating the experience. From what I heard from other friends who had been to that restaurant and had a very similar experience, they don't feel the need to go back either.

Look, stuff happens. You check in for your flight and the agent tells you it's been delayed for forty-five minutes, or it's been moved from this gate to another gate that's a half a terminal away. They changed the equipment and no longer have a business-class seat for you, or you're seated next to the bathroom.

A client was flying to a spa with her sister. The flight was canceled and what was supposed to be a direct flight that took four hours became a three-flight journey that was going to take nine hours. While the airline rebooked the sisters immediately, they put them on different flights arriving at their destination at different times. The two women stood in the line to speak to an agent and asked if there was any way they could be on the same flight. They told him they didn't need to sit together and would pay for an upgrade if that was the only way they could fly together. The agent worked the computer and several minutes later handed the women two sets of tickets for the same flight. Her sister was in fact flying first class, but the agent hadn't charged any additional fees. That's the kind of recovery that cements customer loyalty.

When I'm in a hotel and something goes wrong, I'm the first person to bring it to someone's attention. I assume the management wants to hear from me—or any customer—if there's a problem because they're in the service business. Some years ago, a client on a business trip was staying in a small hotel in Pennsylvania. He asked for a wake-up call, which wasn't made. He almost missed an important meeting. When he was checking out, he mentioned this to the front desk clerk, who comped his room charge for that night.

Unfortunately, not enough people have that attitude, or think they can afford those kinds of gestures. The truth is that losing a customer for life costs you a lot more. I was staying in a five-star hotel in Miami on South Beach where I was orchestrating a large-scale event. My team and I were there for seven days. There were problems checking in, there were problems when I took guests to lunch. The staff was rude and dismissive. I spoke with the general manager of the hotel and was basically ignored. He could have used the information I gave him about how check-in was handled or the problems with the lunch service to make changes that would have improved his future guests' experience. I trust it goes without saying that I no longer use that hotel. Not because I wasn't happy with the way I was treated. Because they showed me they didn't care about customer service, and I didn't want my clients to be somewhere where the manager and staff weren't responsive to their needs.

An apology doesn't have to be formal, but it needs to be sincere and not automated. It should come from a real person to whom your customer or client can respond. A friend ordered a shirt for his girlfriend from L.L. Bean for Christmas. It arrived on time, but it was the wrong color and the wrong size. When he called, he spoke to a live representative who apologized, located the correct item, and told him they would send it priority so it would arrive in time for the holiday. And the incorrect item? Don't worry about returning it.

While I was in living in Los Angeles, I worked with a catering company on a memorial service at a beautiful home in

Montecito. I left after the service and the chef and his staff stayed behind to serve and clean up. Unfortunately, they did not clean the widow's kitchen properly and broke a couple of plates. I didn't know about this until the friend who recommended me called and told me. The first thing I did was to call the widow directly and apologize. I told her there would be a cleaning service there the next morning to detail the kitchen. I replaced the broken plates and sent them with a handwritten note of apology. It was an expensive fix, but the woman was gracious and grateful. And when she started entertaining again, she called and hired me again.

At another event in a client's home, a waiter broke an antique porcelain teapot. I found someone who did the finest restoration work and paid him to repair the piece. I packed it in a beautiful box, carefully nestled in 150 teabags, and wrapped it gorgeously. I had it hand-delivered along with the client's favorite scented candle with a note that said I was sincerely sorry. Even though the piece was no longer perfect and could only be displayed, my client appreciated the effort, and the humor that accompanied it.

Then there was the second birthday party for a client's son. We had hired a clown from an agency with a good reputation. He showed up and had the worst body odor I have ever encountered. We fixed the body odor situation, but he was nasty to the children. They all got very upset, and at one point all of them were crying. I never worked with that agency again. I apologized profusely to the client and did not charge her for the clown's appearance. I've done numerous other events with her, including her fiftieth, sixtieth, and seventieth birthday parties.

•

## Beyond Repair

There are mistakes and then there are catastrophes. It's important to learn to distinguish between the two. Sometimes you can't recover. (In some professions a catastrophe can result in grievous harm or death. That's not the kind of catastrophe I'm talking about here.) In some cases, there's nothing you can do to make things right and keep your customer. That doesn't mean you shouldn't apologize and give them some kind of compensation. As painful as it may be, all you may be able to do is take a long, hard look at what happened and break down how things went wrong. If it was a mistake on the part of you or your team, can you set up new procedures or create a checklist so the same situation doesn't happen again? There was the beachside event where we hadn't thought to check the timetables for the tide. Our team and the on-site staff had to move the tent and furniture to save the event. You can be assured that whenever we do an event on a beach, checking the timing of high tide is on our checklist!

It's never happened to me (knock on wood) but I've heard of events where all the guests got food poisoning. Even if the caterer refunded every penny with interest, there's no way to recover your reputation from an incident like that except by the passage of a lot of time. Unfortunately, in today's world, because of online reviews, it's easier said than done. The bad stuff always sticks to the top. I know people who have done extraordinary work, but when you go online the reviews about the one time an event went badly is the first thing you see on their feed.

A bad haircut grows out, but when a treatment or coloring goes wrong, the effects can be long term and highly visible. It's not the kind of free advertising any of us wants. I know a model whose hair fell out when she tried to go from brunette to ice blond. She lost four months of work. All the free haircuts in the world couldn't get her to go back to that salon or make up for her lost income.

Most of the time, you can recover from a mistake if you apologize sincerely and in a timely way and find some way, even if it's only a token, to compensate your client or customer. If you're replacing a broken item, can you absorb the shipping cost? A friend queried a fragrance company about a late order and discovered it hadn't been shipped. She got an immediate apology, a small size of their most popular scent, *and* a handwritten note with the expedited order. In all the instances I can think of when I or my team was involved and I accepted responsibility and made amends, I still work with those people today.

KEEP IN MIND:

- People complain for a reason. Be sure to put yourself in your customer's place when you're evaluating their complaint.
- We all make mistakes. When you discover you've made a mistake: acknowledge, apologize, assess, assume responsibility, diffuse, recover, and reset.
- An apology should be sincere.
- A complaint or compliment is data you can use to improve your customers' experience.
- Offer your customer some kind of compensation. It's better to take a short-term monetary loss than lose an unhappy customer for life.

NOW ASK YOURSELF:

- Do I have a protocol to respond to and address customer complaints?
- Am I looking at complaints as feedback I can use to improve my product or service?
- Is ignoring or dismissing customer complaints costing me business?

CEO

# six

*Own Your Brand*

T he dictionary defines brand as "a type of product man-ufactured by a particular company under a particular name." The American Marketing Association defines it as "a name, term, service, design, symbol, or any other feature *that identifies one seller's good or service as distinct from those of other sellers."* The italics are mine, because that's the essential part of that definition. Your brand is your identity, and what sets you apart from everyone else in the same commercial space. It's what a buyer or client thinks of when they think of you.

I never went to university to learn how to run a business. I'm almost entirely self-taught and learned through trial and error. The one thing I had no problems with was my brand, because when I started out my business creating events mir-rored how I entertained and lived in my home. I gave my cli-ents the same kind of attention and service I gave to my own guests. Today, Colin Cowie Lifestyle, my events business, and Thrive Hospitality, which focuses on hotel and hospitality consulting, reflect the same qualities of luxury and service I strove to provide when I started out. Those two words guide every aspect of our client's experience, from their first phone call to a meeting in our office through the event itself.

•

## Practice What You Preach

When we serve coffee, drinks, or meals in the office, we use china, flatware, good glassware, and, yes, ironed linen napkins, because that's our corporate brand. Can you imagine how a client would feel if they came to our office for lunch and I handed them a sandwich served on a paper plate with a flimsy plastic fork and limp paper napkin from the corner deli? They wouldn't feel like they've had the Colin Cowie Lifestyle experience, and they wouldn't have. In this business, I'd like our clients to think that we live our lives exactly the same way we keep our offices, and that we'll carry this attention to detail when we plan and execute their events. I don't use the word *perfect* because your best is good enough, but for my clients, I want them to think that what they see is perfect when they walk in the door.

My brand extends to all aspects of my companies' business, including our office design and our business cards and stationery. Even our worksites for events are extensions of the company brand. I insist on an organized jobsite and the production office is completely organized. No one eats, drinks, or smokes on-site; you go outside. There are lists and checklists. There's a Sharpie by the water bottles so everyone can label their own, and there's no waste.

My producers and customer-facing staff represent my company brand. They know that when they travel with me, they dress a certain way. That when you tell someone you'll meet them at six o'clock, you're in the lobby at 5:55. I have a budget for hair and makeup when staff are working an event so they can look and feel their best and present themselves and the company with confidence and style.

We're living in a world of specialists and specialization. (The exception may be Amazon, but being everything to everybody *is* their brand.) The most obvious example may be the medical profession: When was the last time you saw a general practitioner? Even primary care physicians have a specialty. The traditional model of the department store that sold everything from furniture and kitchen equipment to clothing and makeup doesn't work anymore; stores and ecommerce sites that offer a focused and curated inventory are thriving. There was a time when dominant brands like Ralph Lauren and Martha Stewart had product lines in multiple categories outside of their core businesses. If their name was on it, it sold. Today, both Lauren and Stewart have radically consolidated their product lines. Lauren is concentrating on his luxury brands. Martha Stewart is taking her name off products, like paint, that are no longer profitable.

It's a question of trust. The consumer today wants to know that you are playing in your lane. They want to know that you are the best source for whatever they are looking for. Celebrities selling jewelry on the Home Shopping Network that they don't actually wear and didn't design won't fly anymore.

This doesn't mean that you can't grow and diversify if you don't compromise on your standards, stay true to your mission, and are committed and fearless. We created the three divisions of Colin Cowie Lifestyle to serve three separate levels of the event market, while staying true to our brand of providing luxury and service and not compromising our standards. When we launched Thrive Hospitality we took what we had learned in more than thirty years at Colin Cowie Lifestyle in design, event planning, food and beverage service, operations, programming, marketing, and production, and offered it to a new market to help them build guest loyalty and create a signature guest experience. We found that hotels, country clubs, and restaurants all wanted our services.

Hilton is an example of smart brand architecture. Instead of trying to be everything to everyone, they want to be able to offer something in every segment of the market (top, middle, and bottom) *and* be competitive in all of those markets. On the lower end of the price scale you have the Hilton Garden Inns. Next in terms of price and services is DoubleTree, then Embassy Suites, Conrad Hotels and Resorts, and then the Waldorf Astoria Hotels. All the hotels are under the Hilton umbrella, and if you accumulate loyalty points at DoubleTree, you can use them at any Hilton hotel.

Creating a brand and communicating what it is to your consumer requires ruthless editing. It begins with deciding what you are and are not. The Holiday Inn Express hotels offer guests reasonably priced accommodations with limited service and amenities. They may have a laundry room for guests but don't offer room service or an on-site fine dining restaurant, and their guests don't expect it. At the luxurious St. Regis Hotel in New York City, the bathrooms are clad in Italian marble, and there's twenty-four-hour butler service. In addition to the historic King Cole Bar (where the iconic brunch drink the Bloody Mary was invented in 1934), there's a grand restaurant, a suite of glamorous ballrooms, and valet parking. The guests at the hotel expect the highest level of customer service and are willing to pay for it. Both hotels offer guests a place to sleep, but each brand tells their audience what kind of experience they can expect. A guest at the Holiday Inn Express wouldn't be disappointed not to find a bottle of chilled champagne waiting for them at check-in; a guest at the St. Regis might be very disappointed if they didn't find one in their signature suite upon arrival.

•

## Creating Your Brand

Creating and maintaining a brand is essential if you want to thrive. There are corporations that spend tens of thousands of dollars on consultants and focus groups to help them do this, but you don't have to. Follow the five principles below and you can create a brand identity yourself.

1. *Define what you do*, and whether it's better or different from what others in your field do. You can't do everything, and you can't be everything to everybody.
2. *Describe what you do in one sentence.* When you are clear about what you do, and how you do it, you automatically manage your customer's expectations.
3. *Set long-term goals and short-term objectives and decide how to implement them.*
4. *Establish your guiding principles.*
5. *Align your vision (who you want to be) and your mission (how you get there).*

You have a vision for your business. Your vision as a leader comes from you; it is what you want to be and what you want to be doing in the future. It's your *why*. You create your vision statement; it can't be workshopped, even if you refine the language with the help of others. I had a vision for Thrive Hospitality: working with companies in the hospitality space that had been damaged in the post-coronavirus world and wanted to set themselves apart by elevating their customer service, customer programming, and interior design. Our vision statement became: To create a guest experience where one wants for nothing and all senses and services are in harmony with one another.

Your mission is what you're doing now and how it will help you implement your vision. Aligning your vision and your mission keeps you on track to maintain your brand identity going forward.

Your mission statement tells people what drives you to do what you do. It's your *what* and *how*. It's easy to tell someone what you do or what your product is in four or five (or more) sentences, but you've already lost them after the first sentence. The process of getting to that one sentence is invaluable: It forces you to focus on defining your core business and gives you the vocabulary to describe who you are and what you're doing. It becomes the cornerstone for your entire operation, for all your communication and interactions with your customer, and for how you provide them with customer service. It tells them what they can expect when they use your product or service.

Legendary hotelier and former president of the Ritz-Carlton hotels Horst Schulze defined the luxury brand when he said, "We are ladies and gentlemen serving ladies and gentlemen." That simple statement resonated around the world; there's not a hotel executive who doesn't know that story. That statement set a standard not just for the guests, but for the hotel's employees and the hotel industry. It recognizes that everyone in the organization has value, and no matter what their role, the organization respects them and what they do.

I already told you how every employee—even the valets and the cleaners—was empowered to spend a certain amount of money if they could correct a problem or make a customer happy. Every staff/guest interaction is guided by this sentence and is why the Ritz-Carlton maintains their reputation as setting the gold standard in luxury hospitality brands.

Without a vision and mission statement, if you put three different people from the company in a room and ask them what the company stands for or how it's perceived, you'll get three different answers. If you want a team that is heading in the same direction believing the same thing and working for the same goal—and you do—everyone in your organization, no matter how small or big, has to buy in. To do this they have to be invested in the process. I've found that by using the process I describe below, then asking those people what the company stands for, they'll say the same thing. It's your business: the vision is yours. Crafting your mission statement, however, isn't the exclusive province of management. Your mission statement gets workshopped with your team because you want everyone to buy into it. It's not about telling employees what to do, it's about inspiring them in how to do it better. Creating a mission statement may take effort, but the end result shouldn't be complicated. The key is to say what you can in the fewest words possible.

To create the mission statement for Thrive Hospitality, I recruited a cross section of people from different departments. We all sat down and threw around ideas of how we all viewed our mission. Once we had that language, we broke up into groups of two or three. (We're a small company. Your groups may be larger, but I suggest you keep them to eight people, tops. Make more groups if you have to. If you're a sole proprietor, or only have a couple of employees, the principle here is the same.) The groups met for thirty to forty-five minutes and were tasked with crafting a mission statement for the business. When we reconvened, the statements from the majority of the groups said similar things, and the others weren't far off.

It was actually quite easy and organic. Our larger group answered the questions:

*What* is the main purpose of our company?

*Why* do we do what we do?

*What* do we do, and how do we do it?

*How* do we define succeeding at what we do?

We broke up into groups of three to four people to discuss and answer the questions, then reconvened to compare our answers.

For Thrive, the *whys* were:

To help people bring excitement and passion back to their business.

To create a profitable and sustainable business for the future.

To look for opportunity to promote innovation in proactive service.

To create a supportive community to share best practices and inspire one another.

To educate the consumer on the value of our services.

To elevate the incredible potential of the industry through education with expectations of moral codes of conduct.

To create a platform for relationship modeling and merchandising.

The result of our discussions was the mission statement for Thrive Hospitality: *Our mission is to enrich every guest experience.*

Your mission statement is supported by your guiding principles, or core values. Every company needs a set of guiding principles; they're the backbone of a company culture. Your principles or values (how you will be perceived or evaluated by others), when combined with common sense and intelligence, will bring your vision (what you see your business being) and mission (how you want to get there and your purpose) alive.

Your principles could be statements, or you might prefer questions, like the Rotary test for the things they say, think, or do: "Is it the truth? Is it fair to all concerned? Will it build goodwill and better friendships? Will it be beneficial to all concerned?" At NetJets we gave the pilots a stainless-steel card to keep in their wallet with the vision and mission engraved on it. You might consider something like that for your team. If they have to make a decision or are dealing with a customer, it's always there to remind them what to keep in mind.

Like your vision and your mission statement, there should be no verbosity whatsoever in your guiding principles. Personally, I think fewer is better, and shorter is better. Use the least amount of words in each—four to eight is the optimal number. At Colin Cowie Lifestyle, we have seven clear, easy-to-remember principles that say in the fewest words who we want to be, how we want to be, and what we are selling.

**Style:** Distinctive in appearance and form

**Quality:** A high value of excellence

**Integrity and Respect:** Be honest, real, and respectful of everyone

**Passion:** Commitment to the cause

**Intelligence:** Logic, nuance, and understanding

**Grace:** Simple elegance and refinement

**Fun:** Feeling of joy

At Thrive, they are:

**Honesty:** Be transparent and do the right thing

**Caring:** Go the extra mile to truly make a difference

**Innovation:** Be bold and deliver the "wow," but be practical

**Discipline:** Be relentless and consistent

**Reveal opportunity:** Look for what others don't

**Create positive strong emotional bonds:** Inject empathy, surprise, and deep satisfaction into all client touch points

**Deliver value:** Just make it better

**Collaborate:** We work with our clients as one team to ensure commitment and belief

### Maintaining Your Brand

You may feel three or four guiding principles are enough for you. Like the single sentence that defines what you do, focus on the core of what directs you. When you've created your guiding principles, it's important to remain disciplined and not compromise them. Once you regularly allow yourself exceptions, you run the risk of diluting and compromising your service or product. Say one of your stated guiding principles is *integrity*. You tell your customers that your policy is that you don't take commissions from your vendors and pass that cost along to your customer. If you decide to make an exception and continue to do so when you're preaching publicly that you don't, your credibility goes out the window.

Here are some other stellar examples of vision and mission statements and guiding principles from industry leaders; you can find others on the web. They're leaders because they weren't afraid to make a statement about what they wanted to do and then they went out and did it.

At Google, everything the company does revolves around its mission statement. When was the last time you asked Google for something it couldn't answer?

**Vision:** To provide access to the world's information in one click.

**Mission:** To organize the world's information and make it universally accessible and useful.

**Guiding principles/values:** Focus on the user and all else will follow; fast is better than slow, democracy on the web works, you can make money without doing evil, there's always more information out there, and great just isn't good enough.

Microsoft may manufacture hardware and software, but their vison goes beyond their products and expresses the belief in what people make possible. They strive to lead the way into sustainability and to promote diversity and inclusion and transparency in the workplace. Microsoft's mission statement expresses their belief in what people make possible, and these beliefs and values are transferred directly into corporate culture.

**Vision:** To help people and businesses throughout the world realize their full potential.

**Mission:** To empower every person and every organization on the planet to achieve more.

**Guiding principles/values:** Innovation, trustworthy computing, diversity and inclusion, corporate social responsibility, philanthropies, and environment.

Uber may appear to be just a rideshare company, but their mission goes beyond getting people from point A to point B. With their technology, they hope to bring about new opportunities for passengers, helping them meet new people and explore new places.

**Vision:** We ignite opportunity by setting the world in motion.

**Mission:** Transportation as reliable as running water for everywhere for everyone.

**Guiding principles/values:** We build globally, we live locally, we are customer obsessed, we celebrate differences, we do the right thing, we act like owners, we persevere, we value ideas over hierarchy, we make big, bold bets.

Their rival Lyft's vision statement is longer than most and articulates its commitment to the community and people it serves.

**Vision:** Ride by ride we're changing the way our world works. We imagine a world where cities feel small again, where transportation and tech bring people together instead of apart. We see the future as community driven and it starts with you.

**Mission:** To reconnect people through transportation and bring communities together.

**Guiding principles/values:** Be yourself, uplift others, and make it happen.

The ambition and mission of Tesla go far beyond the electric cars for which they're primarily known.

**Vision:** To create the most compelling car company of the twenty-first century by driving the world's transition to electric vehicles.

**Mission:** To accelerate the world's transition to sustainable energy.

**Guiding principles/values:** Doing the best, taking risks, respect, constant learning, and environmental consciousness.

Sometimes there's no real difference between a company's vision and mission; a mission statement is also a declaration of the leaders' vision. Whole Foods, for example, combines them in what they call their purpose statement: "Our purpose is to nourish people and the planet. We're a purpose-driven company that aims to set the standards of excellence for food retailers." Quality is a state of mind at Whole Foods Market. Their guiding principles include: highest quality, all-natural and organic foods, customer satisfaction, promoting the health and happiness of employees and stakeholders, win-win partnerships, profitability and prosperity for all, and promoting community health, nutrition, and welfare. They also lay out specific leadership principles—customer obsession, long-term thinking, people empowerment, learn and grow, giving trust to earn trust, think big, just get it done, and frugality, or accomplishing more with less.

TED (the acronym stands for technology, education, and design) is a nonprofit organization that sponsors short (usually eighteen minutes or less) talks that cover every topic imaginable in over a hundred languages. Their mission/vision statement is brief and powerful: "Spread ideas." In describing who they are and what drives them, they articulate their vision and guiding principles:

> TED is a global community, welcoming people from every discipline and culture who seek a deeper understanding of the world. We believe passionately in the power of ideas to change attitudes, lives, and ultimately the world. On TED. com we're building a clearinghouse of free knowledge from the world's most inspired thinkers—and a community of curious souls to engage with ideas and each other both online and at TED and TEDex events around the world, all year long.

A combination vision/mission statement can work well for small companies. A lawyer's might be, "To provide every accused with the best defense," for example.

●

## Setting Goals and Objectives

Every business needs both long- and short-term goals. What those goals are, how you define long- and short-term, and how often you set and revisit those goals is up to you. We set these goals not just for the company as a whole, but for each department, from IT to the art department, product development, and sales.

Your goals are achieved through your short-term objectives, the smaller steps that are going to get you where you want to be. Breaking down your long-term goals into smaller, more easily attained benchmarks or objectives makes it easier to track your and your team's progress, and to correct course if necessary. On a single event, the goal would be to create an extraordinary event. Making it happen involves a number of different objectives: timely deliveries, more competitive pricing, curated options for the elements of the event.

At Colin Cowie Lifestyle, our corporate goals are:

To become known as a strategic hospitality brand and partner on a domestic and global basis

To be known as the preeminent experiential event-planning company

To create unparalleled experiences by tapping into the five senses

I don't like to dictate department goals. I know what I need to plan a stellar event; I don't necessarily know what my graphic designers need to do their job more efficiently. Instead of management coming to the team and saying to the team that these are your objectives for the year, I prefer to have the team coauthor them. We review our vision and mission statements (more on that below), and I'll ask the group (or in some cases, the one person) to tell me the ten things that would make the department better. It could be streamlining the creative process. It could be rearranging and updating the client database. It could be acquiring or creating new design software. It could be creating a checklist or tracking form that can be accessed by everyone involved in a project.

Decide which objectives should be adopted; you may want to triage your list to keep from overwhelming your team. When a department objective has been decided upon, it's up to the department to decide what sub-objective they can reach by the next meeting and put an action plan in place to get there. It's good if they have to stretch a little, as long as the objectives are achievable.

After your initial meeting you can set up an ongoing meeting schedule. A small organization might set up a yearly meeting to set their objectives and quarterly meetings with all the departments to track their progress. Each department would set a schedule of monthly check-in meetings. A larger, more complex one might need monthly departmental meetings, a quarterly division meeting, and an annual or semi-annual board of directors meeting.

My team meets yearly, quarterly, weekly, and monthly by department. All these meetings have the purpose of keeping everyone on track. It's also a way of keeping us accountable to each other, because what's happening in design and marketing will affect what's happening in IT, and what's happening in IT will affect everyone.

At the beginning of every year, our department heads and I set our goals, objectives, and action plans. These lay out exactly what we need to do during the year. The monthly and quarterly meetings are no more than an hour and a half long. Each person is given twenty to thirty minutes to report on what they and their staff have achieved since the last meeting: what worked, what didn't work, if there were stumbling blocks to meeting their objectives, and what were the successes. After they finish, we have the opportunity to comment, offering feedback, assistance, advice, and sometimes challenging them to make sure that they're fulfilling their benchmarks toward meeting our objectives.

If a person is not meeting their benchmarks or objectives, I want to know why. This isn't about embarrassing or calling someone out; sometimes there's an issue none of us could foresee. Sometimes the team or someone from another department can see a way around a block or problem. Sometimes the reason for not reaching an objective is out of our control, and an event like COVID-19 changes the playing field so we need to revisit and refresh our goals and objectives to get back on track.

For example, when we couldn't find software that matched our way of managing event finances, we asked our IT department to build a piece of custom software for events that we could use to track payments, budgets, and schedules all in one document. You can imagine that when you're orchestrating an event that costs millions of dollars there's opportunity for very expensive mistakes. This system is used by everyone involved in an event, from the producer to the accountants. It has fields that can be reviewed so we can ensure that every step of every procedure is followed, and no one is taking shortcuts. Our company updates let us revisit the software, give feedback on how it's working, and, since we designed and built it, ask for updates (with dates for those updates) if necessary.

Another goal of the department was to find a new system to organize the million-plus images in our database and make them more easily accessible both in the office and remotely so we could respond with customized presentations more quickly. This was a daunting challenge and breaking it into more manageable objectives (creating a sharable database, deciding on a labeling/tagging system, deciding how many images could be cataloged within what period of time, implementing the cataloging in realistic stages) made it doable.

·

## Be Agile

Our goals don't change, but sometimes our benchmarks, objectives, and action plans do. These meetings allow us to adjust and be agile when the business environment changes, or to react to a black swan event like the COVID-19 pandemic.

Look at what happened during the first months of the COVID-19 pandemic. Food wholesalers whose primary business was supplying restaurants opened their virtual doors to consumers. Restaurants sold their stock of ingredients to their customers and pivoted from serving sit-down meals to providing takeout or pre-packaged meals and meal kits. Some auctioned their wine cellars. Distilleries used their equipment to produce hand sanitizer, instead of or in addition to beverages. Clothing companies added masks to their offerings.

In the spirit of the Blue Ocean strategy, being open to change and reinvention, being agile, anticipating, and changing with the market is essential both to understanding and fulfilling your customers' needs and to your organization's survival. Innovating constantly, while staying true to your brand, is a way to keep your customer coming back. You don't have to compete for the same customers as those providing similar products or services if you can create a new market for new customers. There was a time when circuses traveled from city to city. They were all the same: an overwhelming barrage of music, animal acts, acrobats, and stomachache-inducing food. One might be bigger, the other smaller, but not much changed year after year. They were all competing for the same customer with the same ticket prices. Then came Cirque de Soleil, which reinvented the circus experience. Gone were the three rings, gone were the animals. Each year there was a different themed show with original music and imaginative costumes. Performances were housed in a luxurious venue. There was nothing like it. They charged for a luxe experience, and people were happy to pay.

It was during the coronavirus lockdown that an idea that I had been nurturing came to fruition and I started Thrive Hospitality. It used the resources (people and intellectual property) that we already had at our disposal to create something new, and it was also a logical and organic extension of our brand. Although I had been providing these services to several companies over the past fifteen years, this was an opportunity to consolidate our hospitality expertise and consulting options under one umbrella and create a brand. We're currently under contract with three asset managers, and we have enough projects to keep us busy for the next three to four years. We made the most of our challenging circumstances, and you can too. Study your market; a new business environment brings new opportunities. Consider what you have to offer and use the resources—your team, your intellectual property, your existing inventory, your capacity for expansion—you already have. A lawyer or accountant can offer online consultations, just as doctors are expanding their practices to embrace telemedicine. Are you a tutor or teacher? Virtual lessons can be as effective as those in person: I have a friend who is taking online cello lessons. If you were a supplier to other businesses, can you go directly to consumers? Some ranchers and farmers, for example, whose business pre-COVID-19 was primarily selling to restaurants and food service companies, are creating robust ecommerce sites and working local farmers' markets until their primary markets return. And when those markets do return, they will have established another revenue stream.

Is there something you can do to help others find a new way to thrive? The Nature Conservancy bought five million surplus oysters to help struggling oyster farmers. They're not throwing a big party; the oysters will be used to help rebuild reefs and improve water quality.

KEEP IN MIND:

- Practice what you preach. Your brand is what your customer thinks of when they think of you.
- Creating and maintaining a brand is essential to a thriving business.
- Be agile. You can diversify if you don't compromise your standards and stay true to your mission.
- Your vision statement explains why your business exists. Your mission statement tells people what drives you to do what you do and how you do it.

- Your mission is supported by your guiding principles, or core values.

NOW ASK YOURSELF:

- Do I know what my customers think of when they think of my brand?
- Do I have a vision for my business?
- Have my team and I crafted a mission statement? Have we articulated our guiding principles and core values?
- What are my company goals? What am I doing to reach them?

# seven

*Lead with the*

*Best Version*

*of Yourself*

The gold standard of customer service is a top-down experience. You set the tone and expectations of performance for your organization. There's a saying that the fish rots from the head down, and it's true. I find that whenever you see certain behaviors throughout a company—good, bad, or indifferent—invariably they originated at the top. If the boss and people in top management are arrogant and uncaring, you can see the same responses in the people that work for them.

I hate the word *boss*, and I hate it when people call me boss. I'm not a boss; I'm a leader, and I hope that's what you are too. Understanding who you are as a leader means you are able to create the company you want to lead. Not everyone wants to be a Fortune 500 CEO, nor should they be.

We lead by example. We produced an outdoor wedding in Miami that got rained out, and we had to move the reception indoors. Part of the job was transporting the guests from the hotels, and I told the drivers to take the long way around. I improvised rain gear out of garbage bags to protect my tuxedo, and with my good shoes under my arms, and in bare feet, I helped carry the formal arrangements all the way through the gardens in the rain to the new venue indoors. My staff knows I'm not above getting down on my knees to pick up a napkin or clean around the toilet, and they follow my example. Everyone in my organization has graduated from the University of Whatever It Takes.

As the leader of my company, I take a 360 degree approach to my life; I live by the same standards personally as I do professionally. I believe that respect, integrity, and honesty are the tripod that you stand on. If you are missing one of those, you're going to fall.

I used to work out at the gym next to a guy who was always angry. He threw the weights around and was an impossibly difficult person to work out next to. I said to my trainer, "What is this guy's vibe? His energy is so bad." He told me that he was a litigation attorney. He comes in and works himself into an aggressive mood before he goes to work. I wonder what it's like for the people that he works with, and for.

•

## Lead with Your Vision

In chapter 6, I said that while creating a mission statement should involve a team from every part of your organization, the vision for your company and what you want to achieve is yours, and yours alone. Without you, your company is a boat without a captain. If you don't have vision and goals, you're a captain without a map, a compass, or binoculars—going nowhere fast. And if—let's be honest—*when* the shit hits the fan, being a leader means being able to take responsibility and say, "We are in this situation because I made these decisions, and I made these choices. Good, bad, or indifferent, it begins and it ends with me."

Taking on a leadership role doesn't come naturally for some people. Not everyone is cut out to take on the stress or responsibility of being a leader. A lot of people just aren't risk-takers and a leader has to be a calculated risk-taker. If you're uncomfortable taking risks, it may be better to work for somebody else. My business and I went through the economic crash of the eighties. I lived through 9/11, the crash of 2008, and COVID-19. There were many times when I've woken up in the morning and the financial mountain in front of me was so big that I never, ever, ever thought I'd get to the other side. But I did. I thought, "I can do this. I can get to the other side. I might not be able to do everything I need to do today, but I can do something. And I can do more tomorrow. I can do one day at a time. If I can get through one day, I know I can get through the following day. Then I'll get to the third day and the fourth day, and now I've made it to the other side." Slow and steady wins the race.

People are driven by confidence and driven by fear. Confidence is about being bold, being brave, even ballsy. You can't be afraid to knock on doors and ask questions. I believe that when I'm going after an event, once I'm in, I can do whatever I need to do to make the event a success and my client happy. Fear keeps you on edge—in a good way. If you're afraid of losing something you value—your reputation, a client—or not being prepared and making a mistake or failing, you look for the weak spots in your planning or brainstorm how things could go wrong so you have contingency plans in place.

·

## Build a Team

Even a natural leader may lack management or financial skills. If you know you have a weakness in your skill set (and we all do), get help if you need it! Hire the right people. If you're an amazing lawyer with an impressive roster of high-profile clients but you're constantly overdrawn at the bank, it makes sense to hire someone to handle your office finances and payroll. You surround yourself with people to make up for what you don't have. I know very, very well what my skill set is, and I also realize what I can't do. My brain is not wired to understand the intricacies of finance and how it works; I hired two of the smartest people I know to handle my company's finances. Then I did the same thing with our producers: I know what a Colin Cowie party or event should look like and what I want the guest experience to be, but I don't do it every day. I rely on people who can do that and empower them to do it.

Therein lies the key: You don't want to replicate yourself. You plus the people who complement what you do makes a better version of you; again, it's 1 +1 = 3. That person finds two or more people to support and complement their skills until there's an organization of people who each excel at what they do.

You owe it to your internal (the person who sits next to you) and external customers to be the best you can be, a leader worth following. This means treating your staff with respect as you do your clients. It means sharing good news when you have it and bad news if you have to. Sharing good news is easy, and I'm the first to celebrate my team's successes. But when things go south, everyone looks to you. The buck, to paraphrase President Truman, stops with you. My name's on the door. I'm responsible. I'm not a Pollyanna, but I do try to put a positive spin on things. I look for the lessons and opportunities to do better. I also believe my team deserves to be informed about the realities of our business.

We produce massive events for hundreds of guests all over the world. We work with Fortune 500 companies, heads of state, and immensely wealthy clients who have the highest standards. Still, I have a very hands-off management style. I believe part of being a good leader is to empower the people you hired to do what you hired them to do. So many people have control issues and feel they need to micromanage, but that creates bottlenecks, and nothing moves forward.

I respect every member of my team. It's my company, my vision, and I certainly have my idea of how I'd like things to be done. However, I give my staff clear and specific direction, and then it's up to them. I don't breathe down anyone's neck every five minutes, but whatever my team is doing, I expect it to be done better than anybody else. My staff has the leeway to make 80 percent of the decisions involved in their jobs, and they make those decisions on their own.

Learn to listen. If you don't listen, you can't react. If you can't react, you can't be agile. If you can't be agile, you can't pivot. Leadership is looking for the future because every day your competition is looking to see what you are doing and trying to figure out how to do it better. Andy Bryant, former CEO of Intel, wasn't wrong when he titled his book *Only the Paranoid Survive*.

When I talk about the importance of listening, I'm not just talking about listening to your top management team. There are a lot of people who run their businesses this way. Each tier of employees only speaks to the tier above them, and eventually information reaches the CEO or owner. It becomes like the kids' game of telephone, and inevitably the message gets garbled. You listen to everyone in the organization because you never know what someone is going to bring to the table, and you want that information unfiltered. There may be things that haven't occurred to you because your POV is top-down. Your customers are looking from the outside in. Your employees are looking up. They're all seeing things that you may not see. You listen because listening is knowledge and knowledge is power.

When I was first at NetJets, I spoke to everyone in management: the head of the Field Base of Operations (FBOs), the head of owners' service, and the division heads. I learned a lot about how to run a global airline, but I learned how things really worked from the pilots and flight attendants. I often got my most valuable information from the ground crew and the guys who were loading and unloading the luggage from the plane. They're the ones who walked with the clients to their cars and heard them speaking among themselves.

If you're making a case for something, there are things that you want to think about and things you don't want to think about. That was one of the hardest things for me to learn because I always "knew" I had the best idea and was dying for everyone to hear it. You cannot make a sound decision to move a project or initiative forward unless you've asked all the right (and often difficult) questions. I don't believe in giving up on your vision, but when you listen, you hear points of view that can make you think about things you don't necessarily want to think about. I'm the most optimistic person in the world and I think there's nothing we can't do, no matter how outrageous or over-the-top. Stephan Baroni, our president and COO, is the voice of reason. He'll bring me down to earth and balance my enthusiasm with real-world data and information because that's necessary sometimes! I think you have to listen to everyone and make your decision based on as much information as you can get. Almost always, informed decisions are the best ones. Our policies are rooted in sound reasoning and business fundamentals that take into account the big picture, our vision. If and when we need to make changes or updates to a policy, we have a clear understanding of how it was designed to work and what it was set out to do.

There are people who don't like feedback. It gets in the way of their management style. Guess what? That's the selfish ego talking. If you operate on the principle of "my way or the highway," your best people may decide to take a road trip. I once called the CEO of a very big business to give him feedback about what wasn't working in his business and why I wouldn't be using his company's services again. He passed me onto someone else, who happened to be one of the people who had created the situation in the first place. That just confirmed that anything I was going to say would fall on deaf ears, and I was right to take my business elsewhere.

If you want honest feedback and useful information, how do you make yourself accessible? I know a number of CEOs and managers who say they have an open-door policy, but their team doesn't feel comfortable reporting what their boss may not want to hear for fear of reprisal. Think about your management style. Do you only communicate with your direct reports? Do you allow your department or division managers to filter others' concerns? Or do you think that you don't need to be concerned because that's what HR is for? Have you ever watched *Undercover Boss*? The incognito CEO or owner always seems surprised how things are run and how their employees feel about the company and its leaders once they're actually in the trenches with their rank-and-file employees.

I'll always expect and encourage my team to contribute at meetings, but I also like one-on-one conversations. I'd rather go straight to the source. I make it clear to my team that I have a real open-door policy, but I also know some people may not be comfortable initiating a conversation with me. Toward the end of the day, I might walk into someone's office and ask, "What's going on? What are you working on? Is the project going smoothly? Is there something you need that would make things easier for you?" We're not the biggest company, and I may not be the most traditional CEO, but I have a team of happy people, and I know firsthand what's going on in the office and with our jobs. When I talk with my staff directly, a manager hasn't put their own spin on the information and told me what they think I want to hear. I hear from the people who've got their sleeves rolled up and are doing the actual work. They're hearing and seeing things that I'm not seeing and hearing. They speak to the creative partners who would never want to speak to me or my other company officers, the top management. They also speak to our competition. Industry gossip? It's all information.

When it comes to wooing clients or working with our creative partners, I've realized that you don't play a hand of cards without knowing what the other side is looking for or wants. I have learned to wait and listen. I like to ask questions and get the other people talking: What is it that you're looking for? I know there's a competition; what would be the deciding factor in us getting this job? With just a few questions, and in just a few minutes I learn where to focus my attention. Even when there's a conflict or someone's made a serious mistake, I've found it's better to just listen and say, "I'm sure you have an explanation." The information that they give is key to how you respond.

●

## Cultivate Discernment

Discernment, the ability to make nuanced judgments, requires information and attention to detail. I think discernment is like a seventh sense. I try and exercise discernment in every aspect of my life, from deciding which projects to take on to hiring someone new to buying a new vase for my apartment. You know by now that I'm an advocate for ruthless editing, and discernment is part of that process. You need to look at pretty much every area that touches your business—from who you work for, to who works for you, to who are your creative partners, and who represents you, and then decide whether they add or detract from your business and your brand.

As an eternal optimist, I'm a terrible interviewer. This is why I mostly leave hiring new team members to others like my COO. He's instituted a process that relies on discernment at every stage. Say we post a job and get two hundred responses. Many companies have an HR department that's involved in soliciting and screening applicants. Our first level of editing is our IT person who applies certain base criteria to each resume. (If you're wondering why he's the first line, it's because he has a food and beverage background and is a trained chef. He knows the operating model of the candidates' roles we are trying to fill and works well with our hiring team. Having worked for the company for over ten years, he has a good idea of what does and does not work.) If he gets fifty resumes that meet our requirements, he gives them to Stephan. They will go through them together and pick the ten most promising. I think Americans write some of the best resumes in the world. They promise the world, although when it comes to delivery they can be a little thin. We prefer to look for resumes in which people put down what they accomplished in their previous positions, not just what their job entailed. However, even an outstanding resume is no guarantee that an applicant will be right for the job.

Each of those ten people will come in for an initial meeting. If that meeting goes well, they will meet with each division of the company. The head of IT, for example, will want to make sure they have the right computer skills. Our Creative Director (and unofficial queen bee) has an impeccable eye for who will be a good fit for our company culture. Everybody confides in her. Who in your company, even outside of HR or outside the department or position for which you're hiring, can you involve in the process? Then we check every reference. We compile everyone's feedback, and then I'll pick between the top three candidates. In the last five years, only two new hires didn't work out.

Discernment also applies to what projects you take on as a company. I've had someone come to me with what looked like it could be an extremely high-profile, profitable event, but as much as I would have liked (and sometimes needed) that money, I decided not to go forward.

I said discernment is your seventh sense; there are always subtle (or not so subtle) clues if you look for them. Maybe I've been competing against someone else for a big event, and then the client doesn't talk about the budget. They want to change contract terms they already agreed to. They want you to work with their team, not your own trusted creative partners. They keep changing the times and dates of meetings at the last minute. When you research the corporation that wants to hire you and you can't find it listed anywhere or find any information about it with a simple internet search, it's a red flag. I've gone down this road a few times in good faith, but when things don't add up, it's time to save yourself from the headache, and even worse, from the chance of not being compensated as promised.

At least twice a year I've walked away from a project. At this point in my career, if I don't think we're going to have a good journey together, I'd rather not get involved. If a relationship starts badly, it's only going to get worse.

It's important to know when to say no. Recognizing that not everything is meant for you is an important lesson. Even if you need the money at that moment, sometimes taking on a project or contract can cost you more in time, stress—and yes, sometimes in dollars—than it is worth. Being able to say *no* with confidence comes with both understanding who you are as a leader and understanding what your company can and cannot do. It comes from the decisions you've made, the confidence to stand by those decisions, and the ability to stay focused on what it is that you do best. I'd love to do a TV show, but it has to be the right TV show and one that's true to my brand. It has to get me closer to my goal of showcasing my talents and creative energy. I always make an exception for philanthropy, but even then I still practice discernment. I get a lot of requests for contributions. However, when it concerns children, education, healthcare, or art development, I will almost always get involved.

It may be a question of money if you can't realistically give your client what they want for the money that they have to spend. They'll be unhappy with the end result and so will you. I've had clients who were extraordinarily generous to me—sending cases of wine and, in one case, a Hermès diamond watch. But at the second meeting with our producer, the client made this strong, capable, accomplished woman cry. I fired the client immediately, returned the diamond watch, and ended our relationship with the client. We were two weeks into what would have been a twelve-month journey. If he was being abusive to my team at the second meeting, it was only going to get worse from there. Firing the client didn't just protect my team from the client's bad behavior, it sent a strong message to my team that they were more important to me than the bottom line.

I believe you show me who you are by your actions and not your words. I've found that a first impression is usually accurate; people very rarely change. It's never going to get better. Some people say alcohol is the ultimate truth serum, but so is money. You'll find out very soon who you're dealing with when people talk about money and how they wield it.

It's impossible to truly serve others if you don't take care of yourself. We get to choose who we want to be. I am a believer, and one of my prayers is, "Help me to be the best version of myself and help me to present the best version of myself." As in business, you're always looking for opportunities to be the best in your personal life. Presenting the best version of myself starts with looking good. My hair is trimmed, my nails are clean and manicured, I exercise to stay in shape, and I've learned how to eat so that I'm the exact weight that I was when I was twenty-three. My clothes are clean and pressed, and I'm a believer that overdressed is always better than underdressed. I feel good about myself because I choose to take care of myself, and because of that I look good.

•

## Take Care of Yourself

My goal has always been to make a positive first impression. If I tell you I'm going to meet you, I'll be there two minutes early. The moment I'm late, I have to start apologizing. The moment I'm apologizing, I've started our interaction off on a negative footing.

My home reflects that same philosophy. My housekeeper was with me for twenty-five years, but when she couldn't work during the first months of the pandemic you could come into my house at any time without me having to tidy a thing. I washed and ironed, polished the silver, and kept our home immaculate. There was (and is!) always food (and champagne) in the refrigerator. I'm always ready for an unexpected guest.

I use my morning routine to set me up for success no matter what mood I'm in. I set my alarm for 7:00 a.m. and meditate in bed using an app for ten minutes, practice Transcendental Meditation for twenty minutes, and set my intention for the day. I get up at 7:30 a.m. and make the bed. I put on workout clothes and have a cup of hot water and lemon. Only then do I check my phone, go exercise, come back, shower, and get dressed. I eat a healthy breakfast. I start every day that way. I walk into the office with a big smile on my face and greet everyone.

Everyone is different, of course; this is the routine that works for me. Would something like it, or parts of it, work for you too? I didn't have these habits in my twenties; I developed this over time and now it's part of my personal IP. There's something to be said about establishing a routine. Because this practice is so ingrained, I don't have to devote thought or effort to it; I just do it and have so much more energy for the rest of my day.

I think we need to look at ourselves like a car. If you don't stop to rest and refuel, you can't keep going. I work a lot and with many international clients. My clients are located across different time zones, so I have an unpredictable work schedule. I often find myself working late into the night. Those hours come with the business I've chosen. However, I do try and set some boundaries between work and home. I keep my computer in my den, and before I go to sleep, I leave my phone there too. I never take my phone to the dinner table with me. That's the time to sit down, have dinner, and connect with my family and friends. It may not be the same time every day, but there is a time where I go from work mode to night mode. I dim the lights, light candles, and put music on. Most important, I pour myself a very well-deserved cocktail, and I start to prepare dinner.

If you work in an office or have a place of business, it's a little easier to maintain that necessary separation. If you work at home, even part-time, as so many more people are doing since the pandemic, personal discipline and having boundaries is very important. A friend who's a freelance writer sits down at his desk by 8:30 a.m. every morning. He takes a break for exercise at 11:00 a.m., has lunch at 12:30 p.m., and works until 3:00 p.m. He goes for a walk with his partner, comes back, and works until 6:00 p.m. He won't take calls or respond to emails before 9:00 a.m. or after 6:00 p.m. Those are his office hours even though his office is his kitchen table.

I draw bright lines between my work life and personal life. Of course there are times when someone I've done business with has become a dear friend, but those times are the exceptions, not the rule. I'm also very aware that as owner and CEO of my company, I have to be very careful so that no gesture, no matter how innocently intentioned, is misconstrued. One of the ways I keep my lives separate is how I entertain. My home is reserved for my friends. If I'm entertaining for business, it's always at a restaurant or venue outside my home. Any work socializing with my staff takes place either in our offices or at a restaurant, bar, or other venue. I rarely socialize with members of the team alone; it's always with other members of the team.

I'm very careful about how I react and what I say in the office. Emotions are a two-way street—control them or they can get the better of you. My team is there to do their jobs. They don't need to know what's going on with my marriage or my personal life. I'm the CEO of the company. Having a little emotional distance is a good thing, because sometimes a leader has to make hard decisions, and, I think, it encourages respect.

That respect works both ways. Your internal customers, the people at work who sit at the desk next to you, are just as important as the people that come in the door and pay your bills. The relationship between management and their reports is different. Twenty years ago, people shook in their boots when the CEO walked in. Corporate bad behavior was tolerated. People were yelled at and berated in public. Your supervisor could pinch your behind, and you couldn't say anything. Your supervisor could ask you out, and you'd be afraid to say no. People could get away with it. Now, #MeToo has made people accountable. Our world has changed, and in this case, for the better.

Technology is an inescapable part of our lives, but you don't have to let it take over your life. You don't have to be available 24/7. Disconnecting is just as important as connecting! There was a time when it meant there had been an accident or someone had died if the phone rang after ten at night. Now people call, text, or email whenever they want to. I've emailed my team at 3:00 a.m. in the country where I'm working, but they know they don't have to deal with it until the office opens in New York or Los Angeles. A lack of boundaries means you don't have respect for yourself.

I don't charge my phone in the bedroom, so it doesn't interfere with my sleep. I don't leave my computer open overnight. I may work early in the morning and late into the night (and sometimes the wee hours of the morning), but I don't work in the bedroom either.

We could all stand to cultivate a little patience. There was a time when you had to wait a week to see the next episode of your favorite TV show, and if you weren't home, too bad. You'd have to hope for a summer rerun. Now you can binge-watch three seasons of thirteen episodes each over a weekend. We've forgotten to take time to do the things we want to do. We pretend that there are eight days in a week or eighty minutes in an hour. We move too fast to really enjoy what is meaningful: the time to sit down and to have a meal without looking at our phones or computer; multitasking and trying to do too much at the same time, rather than taking the time to concentrate on one thing and do it to the best of our ability.

In 2020, when I was working at home during the first six months of the pandemic, it struck me how much we take for granted and how we unconsciously consume what's around us. We move too fast; instead of enjoying what we have and what we're doing now, we're restlessly moving onto the next thing, looking for something bigger and better. I made a decision to focus more on the important values of gratitude and humility moving forward. I appreciated the opportunity to have the time to look at every aspect of my life and ask myself: *Am I doing my best work? Is this the best version of me? Can I do better?* Of course I can! And so can you.

●

## Finding Support

Being a leader can be a heavy weight, and no one said you had to carry it alone. Ask for help if you need it. I'm a big believer in coaching and counseling and reading. As a self-taught

CEO, I attended the University of Whatever It Takes and majored in Hard Knocks and Falls. My thesis was on How to Get Up Again. I've worked with business coaches and others because I know I still have a lot to learn, and other people have a lot to teach me.

My very first coaching session was when I was nineteen years old with *The Power of Positive Thinking* by Dr. Norman Vincent Peale. It changed the way I thought and taught me to put a positive spin on everything. It taught me that I shouldn't make doubt a part of my vocabulary, and that helped build my confidence. Doubt is not a part of you; it doesn't just happen. You're programming yourself to be positive. I was taught not to use the words *but, if, perhaps, when,* or *maybe* because they're words that allow you to doubt instead of programming yourself to be positive.

If your dog gets sick, you take him to the vet. If there's something wrong with your car, you take it to the mechanic. If there's something physically wrong with you, you go to the doctor. If you have an infection in your business, you find a coach to help you make it better. A coach can give you guidance and tools. It may be your first time dealing with a particular situation, but it's almost certainly not theirs. Why should you make a mistake when you can learn from the experience of others?

Several years ago, I discovered that there was some conflict among several teams in the office. Our healthy corporate culture had slowly and stealthily devolved into gossiping and sniping. I needed help with creating new tools and protocols to rebuild it.

I once had a very toxic relationship with a business partner, and our company suffered. I was in a dark place personally and professionally, and I needed help to get out of it. I had a ball and chain to the tune of millions of dollars of debt after the 9/11 tragedy, and I needed a jump-start to begin to dig myself out of that hole.

As with any business relationship, it's very important who you bring on board in this capacity. You have to do your homework, read all the reviews you can, and then ask to speak to four people who have worked with them. A coach or counselor may have the answers you need, but is it your culture, your way of doing things, your style? Will you be able to follow through? If not, you're throwing your money away.

Commitment and determination are the brothers and sisters that move you forward. Commitment to something means you're going to do it. I often find that committing is the easy part, and the determination to get there is the difficult part. Commitment only works when you have a plan; otherwise it's just lip service. If you commit to something and don't follow through, if you don't accomplish what you've said you're going to do, people will say that you're not dependable.

## Make It Happen

When I was younger, I thought the whole world had to hear what I was going to accomplish. As I've gotten older, I realized it's better to keep quiet until I can announce that I've done what I set out to do. In March 2020, I realized that all of the income from our events division had moved to 2021. It was reason enough to cry. It was cold, it was gray, I was wearing gray, and I felt gray. I lived with my misery for two weeks and then got up early on a Monday morning. I shaved. I got dressed. I fired up Zoom and started to pave the way for what Thrive Hospitality was going to be. I didn't discuss it with people outside the company until we had a complete business plan and launched our website in June 2020. We signed three major accounts in the first three months we were in business.

When you make a commitment on behalf of your organization, your team needs to buy in, because they're the ones who are going to do the work and bring your big idea to fruition. Maybe you have someone who doesn't buy in and has to be on the project anyway (there's always one in every organization). I used to have a business partner who would always give me twenty reasons why something wasn't going to work. I used to say, let's just play "pretend it can work." We can change our minds later.

Determination is the passion that lives inside of you that says, "I can do it. I will do it. I can follow through. I can make my idea come to fruition." Discipline is the self-control that keeps your focus on your goals and helps you persevere when things don't go your way. Determination is very much tied to confidence. You can't be determined unless you're confident, and if you're confident, you need determination and discipline to take your idea through to completion. Confidence comes from previous successes and keeping your promises — doing the things you say you are going to do. You can create a cycle of success by setting up rules that allow you to accomplish your goal. For example, if I know I need to get forty-five minutes of exercise every day, I tell myself that I don't have the option *not* to exercise. If you do this (or anything else) twenty-one days in a row, you'll create a new habit, naturally. If you break down a larger goal into smaller, more attainable ones, it gives you a boost of confidence when you reach each one, and reinforces the determination to reach the next, higher goal. Many people lose confidence in themselves because they don't keep (or can't, if they've overreached) their promises or do what they say they're going to do.

I can't think of anything I do today that's part of my intellectual property that wasn't hard-earned through commitment, determination, and discipline. I had so many things I wanted to do. I was determined to leave South Africa and live in America. I was determined to make myself a success when I got here, and I threw myself in the deep end. I worked in a catering company. I waited tables. I did whatever I needed to do. I wanted to be the best event planner in the world. I wanted a television career. I wanted to appear on the *The Oprah Winfrey Show*, and I was a guest seventeen times. I wanted to be an author, and I'm working on my eleventh book. I committed to those goals, and I was determined and disciplined to do what was needed to get there. Whenever I got off track, my goal always brought me back.

Determination is something that you also want to instill in every team member. Some people are born with it, and some people need to be encouraged and nurtured to develop it. You want to reward it. When we pull off a complicated event or meet a particular goal, we'll bring lunch into the office or go out for drinks. We reward and celebrate our successes, and it all comes back to our organization's culture.

Building that culture is the key to your company's success. We'll look at how you can do this in the next chapter.

KEEP IN MIND:

- It's your vision. You set the tone and expectations of performance for your organization.
- Build a team. Hire people to complement your skills, not replicate them.
- Listen to everyone in your organization. If you don't listen, you won't learn.

- If you don't take care of yourself, you can't take care of your business and your team.
- Cultivate discernment. Know when to say no.
- The qualities of commitment, determination, discipline, and discernment are essential for success.


NOW ASK YOURSELF:

- Am I leading by example?
- What keeps me on track for my goals?
- What kind of self-care routine have I implemented?
- Who are my personal and business support teams?

# eight

*Company Culture Fuels*

*Exceptional Service*

T eamwork, mindfulness, and communication with and among your team are the brothers and sisters of success. You cannot create excellence without them. I think about my mother's story about the spokes of the wheel. When I was drafted into the military, I knew I wouldn't be the tallest, the fastest, and I certainly wasn't the toughest. Before I left for basic training, my mother said, "Look at your life in the army like a spoke in a wheel. Every spoke in that wheel makes the wheel stronger. Every time you do push-ups, you're not doing it for them, you're doing it for yourself. Every time they give you some terrible task to do, you're not doing it for them, you're doing it for yourself, because you can."

I realized that by having a positive attitude, I could strengthen the wheel by making sure that my spoke was as strong as possible. I look at the members of my team in the same way: A single spoke, no matter how strong, can't move a wagon forward. A wheel without the internal support of spokes will break. Put those spokes inside the wheel in the right way, and they are stronger together. If one is damaged or broken, the wheel still functions; the other spokes compensate for the one that's missing. It's another example of 1 + 1 = 3.

·

## The Right People

Surrounding yourself with smart people sets you up for success. Who does your business need? In chapter 7, I told you about *how* we hire, now let me tell you what my team and I look for when we're bringing a new person on board. Hiring the right people for the right job is the smartest thing a leader can do. If you hire well, you don't have to fire.

When we hire, we look for people who have a similar DNA, so to speak, to our company. In our business—hospitality—and at our company, we look for emotional intelligence, good manners, and common sense. We're looking for people who are naturally hospitable; that kind of authentic warmth is not something that can be easily taught, especially in a short period of time. In our business, appearance matters. I'm not talking about good looks or expensive clothes or accessories. We're looking for people who take pride in their appearance and present themselves well. You'd be surprised (or maybe you wouldn't) at people who show up in stained clothes, with chipped nails or bad breath. We're looking for people who are creative, service-oriented, and, to use that old cliché, think outside the box. We're looking for people who *care* about getting every detail right no matter how small. Those little things make the biggest difference. Our COO worked at a restaurant group. When they interviewed a job candidate, they'd hold the interview far back in the dining space when the restaurant was closed for service. The candidate would have to walk through the length of the restaurant to the back. They would drop a napkin in the path the candidate would have to walk. If the candidate stopped to pick up a napkin, they knew that person had the right DNA. If they just walked by without picking it up, they were starting the interview with a black mark against them. Thomas Keller of The French Laundry, one of the best restaurants in the country, lost a Michelin star because one of the incognito inspectors dropped a napkin on the floor during their meal. A waiter walked right past it and didn't stop to pick it up.

This is why interviews are so important. Here are a few of the questions we add to the usual "Why do you want to work at Colin Cowie Lifestyle?" type queries.

1.  If you have a brother or sister, tell me how they would describe you as a person.
    This response provides insight into the candidate's personality and how they fit in at home. Most of the time, they are surprised and amused by the question, and it really helps bring them out of their shell by answering something personal and not work-related.
2.  Tell me about the best day on any of your prior jobs and what made it so great.
3.  Tell me about the worst day on any job, what made it so bad, and what you did about it.
4.  Have you ever been in a situation where a supervisor asked you to do something you don't necessarily agree is the right course of action? If so, describe the situation and your response.

5.  Are there any days you cannot work?
6.  Are you able to travel freely if requested, and how do you feel about travel?
7.  Describe your last greatest challenge in your previous role and how you addressed it.

    We would also ask about their comfort level working in an office and how they would feel about a hybrid working situation.
8.  Tell me about your management style.
9.  Say you bought a new car and you're driving past a bus stop. Waiting for the bus is your best friend growing up (who has saved your life many times), an elderly woman who needs help getting to her medical treatment, and a woman or man who looks like the person of your dreams. You happen to know that the bus won't be coming for an hour, and you only have one seat free in your car. Who do you pick up?

    Most people will pick one person or another, but this is supposed to show how outside the box people can think. The right answer is you pull up, toss your friend the key, and ask them to take the old woman for her treatments while you stay behind and wait for the bus with the woman or man of your dreams. I actually asked this of four people, and only one came up with the right answer immediately.

The exceptional customer experience comes from the bottom up. The person you may think is the least important person on your team can be the most important. I've talked about how the first person your customer meets—a receptionist, a valet, or doorman—shapes the first impression your customer has of your business and can be a valuable source of information about your clients. They can also be a valuable source of information about *you* to your client.

A friend used to go to a frozen yogurt bar in her small town. The food offerings were delicious, but the staff was awful. The owner hired local high school and college kids, which was good for the community, but she neither educated them about service nor supervised them properly. She didn't adjust her staffing so there were more people to cover the busy times. The servers who were there were slow, unenthusiastic, and sullen, verging on rude.

My friend went when the store first opened and chalked up the problems with service to an inexperienced staff who were a little overwhelmed by the crowd. She went back a few weeks later, and there were fewer people in line to be served, but she encountered the same issues. From others she spoke to, the issues persisted. She never went back. The store struggled along for a few more months before it closed. The owner complained that the town made it too hard to do business, but the real problem was that the experience was so frustrating and unpleasant that no one wanted to go there.

As a lot of businesses get bigger, they start to work in silos. No one knows what the other department is doing. They don't have shared goals. Here's a classic example: In September 2020, fitness company Echelon released a $500 "Prime Bike" they said was developed in collaboration with Amazon. Hours after Echelon announced the bike, Amazon denied they had partnered with the company. The CEO of Echelon said Amazon had asked them to develop the bike at that specific price point and said that "even though all the correspondence and the purchase orders call the bike the EX-Prime Bike . . . we learned that an internal Amazon team were not in full alignment." I run a small business (at least in terms of full-time personnel), so it's easier for everyone to see what their colleagues are doing. We have a Tuesday staff meeting to review all of the projects we have in the works. It's a good way to have everybody aligned and share in the same wins and the same fails.

I keep a whiteboard outside of my office that's visible to everyone in the open plan space. On it is a list of target projects, in-progress projects, big to-dos, and contracts that are pending signature. I think of it like a company vision board that keeps us focused on working toward the same goals. This wouldn't work for a bigger company or one with a mostly dispersed workforce, but there are other ways—periodic emails, a shared Google document, other team messaging apps—that can communicate the same information.

·

## Connecting with Your Team

Just as important as your emotional connection is with the consumer, so is your emotional connection to your team. I'm not talking about emotional intimacy here. You can care about the welfare and well-being of the people in your company or on your team without being close friends. I believe that today, as is the case with your consumer, team members will more likely go elsewhere if you're not emotionally connected to them. I know many of the assets in my company walk out the door every night with the possibility that they may not be here tomorrow. It's one of the reasons that, in a crisis like 9/11 or the pandemic, if I'm forced to make a choice, I meet my payroll before I pay rent on the office. Take care of your people because they take care of your business. This means going beyond the basics (fair pay, health benefits, 401[k] plans, safe working conditions) to let them know they're appreciated.

Praise for a job well done is always welcome, and incentives like profit-sharing or commissions over a base salary give your team a stake in the success of your business and their income.

Culture is the fuel of your business. You know you have a good company culture when everyone is accountable, and they understand their roles and the difference that they make individually and as a team. They'll come in early and stay late if they have to. A good culture comes from leading by example and by listening. It comes from creating a good working environment. It comes from rewarding your people in ways that are meaningful to them. It doesn't always have to be a monetary reward.

Once a month at our weekly Tuesday meeting, we have a little ceremony called "pass the baton." I started it to recognize a team member who had gone above and beyond in their job and supporting their team members in some way. The next month, that person identifies someone else on the team that they feel deserves to be recognized and tells us why. It shines a spotlight on that person and their accomplishments, and during the meeting we tell them what they mean to us and why they're valuable to the company. The next month *they* get to pass the baton, identifying someone they believe deserves to be recognized.

I'll bring in lunch for everyone at the office for no reason or start off a late afternoon creative meeting with wine or cocktails. Obviously if you have a hundred (or more) employees drinking on the job, that isn't appropriate and isn't a good idea. Could you give members of your team the day off for their birthday? Empower a department head to bring in breakfast (or lunch or dinner) for their individual teams?

In my events business, it can mean giving a producer who's working on a high-profile party an allowance for a new dress and shoes. As I mentioned earlier, I bring in hair and makeup for the women working an event so they walk out on the floor with confidence and feel as special as the guests do. They're representing the company and our brand, and I want them to look their best in their job and do it with style.

We publicly recognize and celebrate our successes. I like my team to feel that they're invested in the success of the company, not just their own projects. Each time we close another deal or have a big win, I crank up the music and let the whole office know so all can share in the success. As soon as there is a free moment, we meet in the conference room or local bar to celebrate. The music may be a little corny, but that's part of the ritual and part of what makes it fun. The night before an event, we host a dinner for the staff and creative partners (on the company dime, not the client's). It raises morale and gets everyone aligned to work together to produce a successful event.

On the lighter side, our office is always provisioned with good coffee, snacks, and a well-stocked bar for impromptu after-hours company get-togethers. If you don't think good coffee is important, let me tell you a story. A young woman I know worked for a small law firm. The partners noticed that staff was going out for coffee during the day, and they were concerned about the amount of time they were away from the office. They put a coffee machine and a supply of coffee in the kitchen and considered it one of the perks of working for the firm. After two weeks, they noticed no one was drinking the coffee, and they were throwing out a full pot at the end of the day. When they asked one of the paralegals why no one was drinking the coffee, she said bluntly, "It's bad." They made the investment in improving the quality of the coffee and provided real milk. Those kinds of small gestures go a long way. It was a win for the employees, and the partners. It showed the staff that their management took their feedback seriously and it cut down the time that people were out of the office.

As a leader you're walking a fine line. It's important to respect employer-employee boundaries and still find ways to create a personal connection without ever getting personal. I make sure that I stay in touch with my team through food and drink, in bars and restaurants, and talking about culture. Especially in those situations, there's enough to talk about without crossing inappropriate lines.

There are also concrete ways to create a company identity. Branded gear such as hats, shirts, jackets, backpacks, computer bags, and name tags are simple and effective ways to identify people as part of your team. Jake, from State Farm, in his simple red sweater and khakis, is immediately recognizable as a brand representative. At a gas station, this could be as simple as having the attendants wear T-shirts with the company logo. At NetJets, we gave every pilot a box of branded gear as part of the employee onboarding process. There was a jacket with your name badge on it and your lanyard with your identification. There was a baseball cap and water bottle with the NetJets logo and a bottle of sunscreen. There was also the stainless-steel business card with the vision and mission statements that I mentioned in chapter 6.

## What's Your Culture?

Because I'm in the hospitality business, my offices are representative of our company culture. Everything from the interior design, to how we greet a client, to the way we serve coffee or tea represents who we are and tells our clients the level of service, attention to detail, and style that they can expect from us. It's the same for our team members. Even when we don't have clients coming to the office and it's a "casual" day, everyone is well groomed. You don't come into the office unless you've taken care with your appearance. A creative partner came in for a meeting and met one of our producers coming up in the elevator who turned to her and said, "Is this a good messy bun, or is it just a messy, messy bun? I can't go to my desk if it's just messy." She assured the producer her hairstyle looked intentional.

There was a time when job-hopping every couple of years was frowned upon. Today I've found it's rare for people to stay in one place for more than two or three years. We want to stop that revolving door because every time one of your team leaves, it's very disruptive and they leave with a bunch of your intellectual property. Places like Apple and Google have built campuses that cater to almost every physical (I said *almost*) need, covering everything from dry cleaning to day care, restaurants, and laundry. We can't all be a tech giant, so how do you build a company culture that retains your best employees?

An open-door policy encourages honest feedback from our team and the opportunity to address problems. I and my upper management are always ready to listen to concerns or problems that our team brings to us. I want to hear from people directly about their concerns and how they think we can do better. I know I need to surround myself with people who ask the hard questions—questions that I may try to ignore because I'm an optimist. I don't care whether those questions come from my COO or our newest intern. I want my team to think, question, and make me think and question too.

I believe in investing in the people who work for my company. I want to nurture and reward talent. When I was working with NetJets, I would meet with different groups in the organization. I would tell them, "Don't think that the skills you're learning are only going to benefit you here on your job. These are things that will make you better parents and will help you to run a better, more efficient home. You can use them socially. What I want to teach you is to be a better version—no, the *best* version, of yourself." I want to do the same for the people who work with me. Whenever I've had to part ways with someone, they've always come to me and thanked me for all the things that they learned while they were with the company: how to conduct themselves so they were comfortable in any situation, how to travel, how to take notes, how to write a proper thank-you note and how to be.

I know annual reviews have a bad reputation. People hate doing them as much as people hate receiving them. And let's be honest: the nuts, bolts, and mechanics of a review are pretty much the same everywhere. Where I see the difference in what we do is that I look at reviews as opportunities for staff development, a way to give *constructive* criticism to our team, and to hear back from them as well. We address areas where we see someone underperforming and give them specifics about where we see weaknesses and what they can do to correct them. We're just as specific when we're highlighting super performance. In our organization, what's said at a review shouldn't come as a surprise because our team gets constant feedback and guidance during the year. If a team member is surprised by their review, something's gone wrong with the communication between them and their manager, or their manager hasn't been doing their job.

●

## The Buy-In

The way to ensure the best and most consistent customer service is to have everyone on your team buy into your company culture. When your team has a hand in shaping your mission statement and establishing company goals, they have an emotional investment in putting them into practice. I explained the *how* behind this in chapter 6, but the *why* is important to strengthening your company culture. When I hand my team a piece of paper with our mission statement and guiding principles and say, "Here's how we do things," it's a mandate. It's something they've been told to do. On the other hand, if you just guide them, when your team writes that statement and delineates those principles, they own them. The company DNA becomes part of their DNA, and an internal guide to fine-tune what they do going forward. The mission statement and guiding principles form the blueprint of how every member of your team operates from and is the bedrock of your company culture.

This is why I don't like to talk about "training" my team. I educate them. Training is tactical: it's for the military and service dogs. The distinction is particularly important when you're working with today's young workforce. They ask questions, and they're not afraid to challenge the rules and say, "Why not?" They're smart, even if they may not be polished. You could say that we install the software to get them up to speed.

When people are customer-facing, teach them how to read customers' body language and give them the skill set and tools (combined with common sense) that will allow them to deliver the right service gestures. Remember the spa experience I shared in chapter 3? The well-meaning staff who kept interrupting me to ask if everything was okay had been trained instead of educated on how to read and respond to a guest's mood and needs. I didn't leave that hotel, but there are circumstances that could cost you your business.

When someone leaves the company for a position with more responsibility and better pay, we wish them luck and success. Inevitably, you are going to lose people. Even then you have an opportunity to transmit your company culture. One young woman in our organization was offered another position and wouldn't tell us if she was going to stay or leave for almost two weeks. When she finally decided, she told our COO because she was too embarrassed to tell me. She left the next day. Very bad business practice. How you end one project or job is how you start the next one. You're creating career karma. I wasn't surprised when a month later she called and asked for her job back. She said she'd made a mistake.

I told her she made two mistakes: the first was leaving, and the second, much worse mistake, was how she left. I didn't say this to be mean or vengeful, but I wouldn't bring her back because I couldn't trust her not to do the same thing again. It's like any relationship. If you break up and get back together, maybe there's a grace period when the other person is on their best behavior. I've observed that most of the time they'll behave the way they did before. There have been a couple of cases where someone left and later came back, but only a couple cases in thirty-five years. They left for the right reasons and in the right way. There are exceptions to every rule.

YOU CAN MAKE A DIFFERENCE in the world. Weave giving back into your company DNA and your mission. It doesn't matter whether it's on a local level (sponsoring a school garden) or global level (a buy-one, give-one program). Encourage employee initiatives and support volunteer programs; match your employee's charitable contributions. I feel strongly that we all should give to charitable causes whether you're donating time, goods, services, or money. I believe that what we give comes back to us tenfold. It's part of our moral compass to take care of those who have less than we do. I have my personal causes—charities

like Lalela and Ubuntu Pathways that serve children and promote education and art education. They are based in South Africa and will always be close to my heart. I support them through
company efforts like our corporate Christmas gifts. I also encourage individual efforts and contributions. If someone comes to me
and says they want to work in a soup kitchen or help paint a
school or community center, I'm happy to give them time off.

I'm going to get up on a little soapbox here. There is no tradi-
tion of philanthropy in the world greater than that in the United
States. It's part of the fabric of this country. I've tried to raise
money at a fundraiser abroad. In a room full of the wealthiest
people in the country, I could finish the evening with $100,000.
In the United States, it would have been a million. Look at Facebook's birthday fundraisers: they almost always exceed the
amount their sponsor is asking for. Amazon offers customers the
option to support a favorite charity with every purchase. I believe
that mindset is exclusive to America.

Give your staff the right tools. As I mentioned earlier, we
have a "bible" of protocols, flowcharts, scripts, and rules on
everything from greeting clients to how we deal with each new
event. These are the essential components to getting everyone
up to speed and in sync quickly. When we hire a new team
member, they receive an onboarding document that welcomes
them to Colin Cowie Lifestyle, and lays out our vision, mission
statement, guiding principles, and values. They receive an employee handbook that covers everything from appearance
standards to benefits and vacation policy. We walk them
through company procedures for setting up meetings and
maintaining our working environment. Our conference and
protocol manual leaves nothing out, even providing pictures
of how we lay out our coffee or tea service for guests or set the
table for a working lunch. It may seem excessive, but service

is our brand and part of our culture, and this level of detail guarantees consistency. By having these standards in place and codified, anyone in the office can take on a task at any time and do it correctly. Even if you have five people in your organization, having some kind of onboarding documents and a handbook of procedures and expectations is essential to integrating new hires into your company culture.

This level of attention to detail and consistency is an integral part of our business when we do events. The protocols and checklists help protect what we've created. Standards and consistency equals predictability and reliability.

Your goal is to have a consistent, reproducible protocol for handling different situations, and to allow your staff to use their own initiative and instincts when necessary. For example, we created a flowchart for each potential sale with sequential steps, a place to check off completed tasks, and comments. It begins with the inquiry and response. The next goal is to set up a call to gather information and then an in-person meeting, if possible. The next item on the list is to use the information to customize our presentation, and after the meeting, to make sure we follow up. We have flowcharts for other areas of the business as well. Each event or production has its own highly detailed flowchart or checklist that is accessible in Dropbox to each person involved. There's nothing left to chance. It allows us to get everybody on the same page at the same time, working toward the same goal: success.

We've all spoken with a customer service representative or had an online chat where it was clear that the person on the other end of the conversation was reading from a script. Scripts reflect the culture of the company that creates and uses them. Like other automated responses, they are most useful when the same situations arise over and over again. In many simple situations, a script will suffice to ensure an efficient and pleasant customer interaction: an item needs to be returned or there's an error on a bill that's easily corrected. You can program variations into a script that give your team limited choices in their responses but still create an emotional connection. In chapter 4, I noted the Chewy customer service representative who sent flowers and a condolence note when a customer called to return food after their pet had died. In a similar case, the customer service rep arranged to send a painting of the customer's deceased pet. Both responses reflected the company's internal culture of caring and compassion and allowed their customer service team to use their emotional intelligence to create an authentic response to the situation. With those unexpected and caring responses, the company created a strong emotional connection. When both customers brought new pets into their homes, they went back to Chewy for all their supplies.

However, if there was a more complex issue and the service representative either couldn't or wasn't permitted to answer your question or address your problem, you probably got off the phone angry or frustrated. You knew you were getting the automated response, and that's not real customer service. I've never been a believer in verbatim scripts because it puts people on autopilot. I like to role-play with my team to hone their response skills. We start with your basic "Good morning," and then I have them tell me what they see and hear. Am I an angry person? A happy person? An impatient or rushed person? A shy person? You would respond differently to each one.

Participation in role-playing scenarios that combine skills and common sense helps prepare your team for different situations. I also find role playing useful in team building. Let's look at NetJets again. The pilots would get on the plane and make a left-hand turn into the cockpit. Once they were there, they didn't give another thought to what was going on behind them because they didn't come from a customer service mindset. They didn't have respect for the support team and what they did. I would have them play "A Day in the Life Of." The goal was to get people in positions of power to have a better understanding of another person's job, even one they thought wasn't particularly important, and learn to respect the other person's role. I had the pilots take the role of the flight attendants and the flight attendants take the role of the pilots. Now all of the sudden, the pilot, who thought all the flight attendants did was serve coffee, is struggling with explaining safety training and procedures. They were wondering what to do when the catering didn't arrive; do they improvise with what they can find, or do they have time to run to the store? The pilot hasn't had to think about how to get the passengers safely off the plane if it lands in water, and now he does. When that exercise was finished, they had a better understanding of the knowledge the attendants had to master and what their job really involved. I've done the same kind of exercise in the sales office of a luxury apartment building. I had the valet and the head salesperson switch roles.

Everyone who participated in these exercises struggled. That was the point. I love the word *struggle*. It's only when you struggle that the lessons stick. You can't create the 3x5s for your team and say go do the 3x5s. The team needs to watch each other do the 3x5s and critique each other's performance. If they don't hold each other accountable at every turn, within two months or less, those protocols will be forgotten. You don't hand someone a script and expect them to internalize the information. Show me, struggle with it, and that repetition makes it stick.

I see scripts as a template for customer interactions that can be customized by each team member, using their own judgment about what is needed for a particular situation. It's what we did with the pilots at NetJets and can be applied to dealing with any client or customer. We told them how to address clients but also taught them how to read body language so they could tell, for example, whether the client wanted to have a conversation or be left alone.

In my personal experience, I was gifted three days at an expensive oceanfront resort and spa in Montauk at the beginning of the season. When I checked in on Friday afternoon, I was taken to an annex far from the main building that looked so inviting on the website. The room was small, musty, and though the finishes were fresh, it was very dated and only had a partial view. When I turned on the ancient air conditioner, it sounded like an airplane was about to take off. There was no shelf in the bathroom to hold a razor or toothbrush and toothpaste. I called the front desk and asked if I could be moved to a room closer to the main building, and if possible, with an ocean view. The person at the front desk told me they would see what they could do. I didn't hear from anyone again until I got a text late Sunday afternoon asking if I would like to move to another room. That was autopilot. The gold standard of service would have been to have someone call me on Saturday to explain the situation, even if a room wasn't available, and let me know what the status of my request was. A gracious gesture would have been to offer an upgrade the next time I came to the lodge, a complimentary spa treatment, or even a drink or dessert with dinner at the restaurant, encouraging me to return.

In order to feel confident using their own judgment, your team can't be scared that there will be retaliation if they make a mistake. I was seated next to my friend and legendary CEO of the Blackstone Group, Steve Schwartzman at a dinner party in St. Tropez.

I asked, "What is the one lesson I could learn from you?"

He said, "Empower your people to make 80 percent of the decisions. Too many business owners, managers, and directors tend to hold on and micromanage so much that things don't move forward. I've often said to my team that sometimes your best is enough." I had a lovely team member who once spent three hours looking for the perfect $1 amenity bag. That's a decision that could have been made in five minutes and took her time away from far more important tasks on a time-sensitive project. Look at the big picture, set priorities, and don't waste your time trying to achieve perfection; it's not possible.

"What about mistakes?" I asked.

He said, "If you hire well, usually people make one mistake and they learn very quickly not to do it again."

It's part of our culture that we all learn from each other and each experience. You don't learn when you only capitalize on your successes. You learn from your mistakes. Those are the things that make you vulnerable. I do a SWOT analysis, which asks the questions: "What were our successes? What were our weaknesses? What were the opportunities? What were the threats?" It's all about making each team member accountable and getting into the mindset that I screwed up last time so I'll do a much better job this time. And it's not just, "I screwed up." It's, "This is what I did wrong, and this is how I can correct it next time." It may be having an additional production meeting, double-checking X, Y, or Z, or speaking to X person before the event and making sure that they have done X, Y, and Z. Then we don't make that same mistake again. As your team grows and learns, remind them that this type of critical thinking can be applied to other aspects of their job.

Of course there are mistakes, and there are failures. I'll talk about why we all need to fail in order to succeed in the next chapter.

KEEP IN MIND:

- Surrounding yourself with the right people sets you up for success.
- Your emotional connection to your team is just as important as your emotional connection with your customer.
- When your team has a hand in shaping and establishing company goals, they buy into implementing them consistently.
- Your company culture is the fuel for your business.

NOW ASK YOURSELF:

- Am I giving my team the right tools to set them—and my company—up for success?
- What am I doing to invest in the people who work for my company?
- Am I taking the time to educate my team, or am I training them?

# nine

*Failure Is a*

*Necessity*

As Beyoncé said: "The reality is, sometimes you lose. And you're never too good to lose, you're never too big to lose, you're never too smart to lose, it happens. And it happens when it needs to happen. And you have to embrace those things." She's right.

Failure is both an inevitability and a necessity. In business and in life, things very, very rarely work according to plan. You can't beat yourself up every time. If you're going to stay in business, you have to know how to find the light in the dark. Every time we're dealt a blow, big or little, we have the opportunity to learn and develop resilience. Michael Jordan said, "Failure is just an obstacle on the road to success. It doesn't matter how many times we fail at things, as long as we've had the courage to try and can muster up the courage to try again."

We ask ourselves: How do we come back? How do we come back stronger? When everything goes our way, why would we ask those questions?

Failure is an integral part of success. We have one process in mind, but when something else happens, you often discover the magic along the way. When you think about it, there aren't any mistakes. A mistake is our selfish ego wanting something to work one way—our way. If you have the right mindset—and I know you do—you'll look at every failure and find, well, not the silver lining, but something—a lesson, a new idea, an opportunity—that you didn't have before.

There are three kinds of failures:

1.  You screw up or your team screws up.
2.  You try something new and it goes wrong.
3.  Something comes out of left field and everything blows up.

No matter *why* there is a failure, if you take the time to analyze what happened, you will be able to reset, possibly recover, and in some cases, pivot to find a new way forward.

Often we fail because we make assumptions. Making assumptions means we haven't really done our homework, and we're willing to leave things to chance. That's not setting yourself up for success. As Ronald Reagan said, "Trust, but verify." I've created checklists and protocols so my team and I *avoid* making mistakes. When we meet to discuss a project, if an item hasn't been ticked off the list—a follow-up call or thank-you note hasn't been sent, a creative partner hasn't been contacted—we know what has to be done and who has to do it. It's why we create such detailed lists for each event. I've found just the act of writing down something helps fix it in your mind. (There's real science behind this: when you take seven seconds to focus on something, you don't forget it.) We don't assume that any one person can keep the thousands of details needed to make an event extraordinary in their head. And there's always the *what if.* What if the florist is stuck in traffic? What if the bride tears her dress? Do we have a Plan B? Do you?

No matter what product or service you provide, there are a million things that can go wrong. When one of my clients tells me that they want the perfect event, I tell them that they came to the wrong man. I can't do perfect; I can only give you my very best.

Stuff happens. Nobody fires on all cylinders at all time. Checklists and protocols can protect you from most mistakes, but not all. In my business, my team and I have to plan for uncooperative weather, equipment that doesn't arrive, IT glitches, travel issues, and client meltdowns, to name just a few. I've always told my clients that if there's a problem I will fix it before their guests notice. Many things *will* go wrong, and they'll never even hear about them.

On a walk-through of a tent venue a few days before an event, our client noticed that the elaborate swagging was no longer in the ceiling. My producer assured him we were just making a few adjustments. What she didn't tell him was that the fire inspector had made us take it down, even though we had already obtained all the proper approvals. We had forty-eight hours to buy new fabric, flameproof it, and construct and install the new swagging. The client was none the wiser.

This is one of the reasons writing those detailed check-lists is so important. Often, going over those lists either on paper, digitally, or in your head can prevent an omission or error from happening. When it doesn't, that's why you want to surround yourself with an amazing team of proactive people who can hit the *reset* button to make sure that you're back on track.

I think the easiest failures to recover from are the ones that are your (or your team's) fault. An example would be when you make a mistake in delivering your product or service to your customer. I didn't say that the process of recovering wouldn't be painful because it usually is. In these cases, you made a mistake, and you need to fix it. The ball's in your court to come up with a solution that will regain your client's trust and confidence.

If your clients know you're as good as your word, that if you say you will do something, you will do it, then it's much easier to recover from a mistake because they know you will do what you can to make it right. If your clients lose their trust in you, you've got a long road ahead to earn that trust and their dollars back. I had a producer who tried to be a star salesperson but didn't follow company protocols when she tried to improve the profit on an event. The client, a very smart and savvy businessman, looked at the bills and questioned them. Instead of apologizing, accepting responsibility for the problem, and correcting the charges right away, the producer blamed the supplier. The client called me and said, "I'm sorry, Colin. I like you personally, but I can't do business with your company." It wasn't my fault directly, but it was my responsibility. We lost the event. I was devastated, but I understood. We had violated his trust.

This makes me think of a show I've been watching about the Vikings. What struck me was how much emphasis they put on reputation and honoring one's word. When one of the Viking earls allies with the king of Wessex, the king promises him land for his people to settle on. When the king dies, his son honors his father's grant. Back then, a man was only as good as his word, and if he ever went back on it and lost the trust of his allies, it was essentially a death sentence. Today, people will say almost anything to make a deal. A broken promise may not kill us, but it can certainly ruin our reputation and kill our business.

I always advise that if you're going to make a decision, base it on as many facts as possible. Use data and logic to come to a conclusion. No matter how much research and how carefully reasoned your decision, you can't be right 100 percent of the time. Maybe you made a bad investment. (Could you have researched the company more thoroughly?) Maybe you bought the wrong printer for the art department. (Should you have spoken to the team about their needs before you made the decision?) You bought a new brand of cheap nail polish and half your clients have an allergic reaction. (Was saving some money worth the hit to your reputation?)

Remember New Coke, also known as Coke II? It wasn't that the executives at Coca-Cola didn't have the data to support their decision to replace the original formula in the spring of 1985. They just underestimated the intense attachment Coke drinkers had to the original brand, and that attachment was fierce. People were hoarding cans and bottles of the original Coke. By June, the company was getting eight thousand calls a day from disgruntled Coke drinkers. (Did you know that 1.7 *billion* servings of Coke are consumed every day? I'm surprised they only got eight thousand calls a day. Can you imagine what would have happened if Twitter had been around?) That summer, company executives called a news conference to apologize and announce that the original Coke would return. When it did, the company regained the market share they had lost, and their market position actually became stronger. And New Coke? It was retired in 2002 and had a limited rerelease in 2019.

●

## Prepare for the Unthinkable

Sometimes failure isn't the result of anything you've done or could anticipate. We've all been in situations where the problem was something out of our control or someone else's error. The officiant didn't arrive on time. The smoke machine broke. We're at a remote venue and the electricity goes out; the backup generator doesn't kick in. When these things happen, we take full responsibility because it happened on our watch. It doesn't matter that it wasn't our fault, but at the end of the day, we are equipped to do something about it.

I saw a meme that said, "Can we all agree that in 2015 no one got the answer right to the question 'Where do you see yourself in five years?'" If you weren't working in the intelligence community or at the CDC, I doubt anyone would have expected a global pandemic that devastated the world economy. However, it seems to me that the global disruptions have increased in frequency over the past twenty years. During the COVID-19 pandemic, it was estimated in New York City that 40 percent of small businesses would ultimately fail and 60 to 80 percent of non-chain restaurants might not reopen. Airlines cut capacity, some by up to 80 percent, and in the US, Virgin Airlines filed for Chapter 15 bankruptcy protection. It was estimated that 50 percent of the world's airlines would not fly again. Brick-and-mortar retail and the traditional bastions of luxury goods and over-the-top gifts have had to do things very differently. When I spoke to my colleagues in the events business in the ninth month of the pandemic, 98 percent of their business had been postponed, some by a year or more. If you wanted to do business in the future, you had to find a new way to maintain some kind of income stream going forward.

Recovery can come out of failure, and sometimes that recovery can pave the way for even greater success. When I returned to the United States after my honeymoon in the spring of 2020, I expected to have the busiest spring in years. I was going into production on a new television show centered around Colin Cowie Lifestyle, I had speaking engagements set up around the world, multiple events in the works, and, of course, I was writing this book. Then the world changed, and life as we knew it was disrupted completely. I watched business and potential earnings fly out the window. All of our scheduled events moved to 2021 and so did much of my income.

"What do I do now?" I wondered. I could sit in my apartment and wait for the phone to ring. Or I could ask myself, "How do I turn failure into success?" While I and my business are best known for producing spectacular events, part of my business has always been consulting for hotels and other hospitality-based venues, creating extraordinary guest experiences and often taking on the role of creative director. I'd been strategizing the creation of a hospitality-based division of Colin Cowie Lifestyle that could supply a more consistent income stream. It would mean we could be less dependent on the events busines (which had become so saturated with people providing services for less money). Because of the volatile and unpredictable nature of the events business, my team and I never had the time and opportunity to sit down and define that company identity and its offerings, as well as determine our core audience. I had a vision, but we hadn't had the time to workshop a mission statement or guiding principles. When our country went into lockdown, CCL had nothing except exactly what I needed—*time*! Now I had the chance to make my dreams become reality.

We spent the next sixty days doing just that and that's when Thrive Hospitality was born. I can honestly say that it was during my darkest moment that I created one of the brightest lights.

Experience is a great teacher. For me personally, 2007 had been an amazing year: I was launching another book, had a multimillion-dollar hotel project in Hong Kong, multimillion-dollar parties going on all over the world, had a successful product line on Home Shopping Network, and then decided to build an internet wedding business that was going to be the Big Disrupter. What could go wrong?

In true Colin Cowie style, we didn't start small. In a short time, we had raised $10 million and brought in talent to build the website and create content. Expensive talent. With of all that going on, I was also building a home that would be valued at $7.5 million.

Then came 2008, the perfect storm—not only for me, but the world. It reminds me of a friend at the time who said he felt as though he was a goldfish in a bowl, saying, "What water?" I hadn't yet exhaled and had just created one of the world's biggest parties for the opening of Palm Island in Atlantis, Dubai. A picture of that event became the cover of *Newsweek* on the first of January 2009 with the headline: *Is the party over?*

*Yes, what water?* Talk about a wake-up call.

The first thing I did that day was make sure the final check from the client had cleared at the bank. On January 3, my birthday, the bank decided that they weren't going to approve my mortgage application. (No need for a thank-you note to a mortgage lender!) If work on my new house was going to continue, I would have to pay for it myself. Eventually I did get a mortgage, but my monthly payments were more than triple what I had anticipated.

Everything went wrong that could possibly have gone wrong, and as you can imagine, it all came tumbling down. Work came to a grinding halt. The internet business was bleeding money. Every big party or event that I had scheduled was canceled. My deal with NetJets was canceled, because now "luxury" was a bad word. My hotel consulting came to a halt because all of a sudden there was no money globally. I figured that we'd be able to ride it out and in six months we'd all be back again. Of course, I was wrong. The fact that there were so many other businesses going through the same implosion didn't help me to feel any better. I had no idea how my company and I were going to get through this.

Two things became very clear: one, I had to get control of myself, and two, I had to manage my finances. As painful and difficult as it was, we reduced a staff of sixty hardworking, dedicated people to sixteen. With the help of my accountant, we cut every business expense possible. I negotiated a payment schedule with the IRS for my taxes, extensions with the bank on my outstanding loans, and deals with my creative partners to whom I owed money. I told everyone that I can give you a check now, but I'll go out of business. Or we can work out a payment plan. I was fortunate and grateful that all my creditors agreed to work with me.

It was a very, very tough time, but I held my head high and did the right things. That year, I was also ending a twenty-year relationship. I felt like hell, but every day when the elevator door opened, I walked into the office with a smile on my face and would greet my staff with, "Good morning, everyone. We're going to make it a great day today." And some days we did. I got this job, and then I got that job. At the end of the day, I paid back every cent that I owed to everyone. What a great feeling.

There were days where I paced up and down my hallway at work and living room at home thinking about what my next move could be. If I did this, how could I do that? If I did this, what would the ramifications be? I knew that I had to be positive and make it to tomorrow. Doing that, I could make it to the next day. And then the following day. It was mental exercise placing one foot in front of the other and trying to stay balanced through meditation. There were days I thought, "I'll never get through this."

I'm grateful and fortunate to have unbelievably supportive friends who believed in me, advised me, and cheered me on. That 2010 brought me the opportunity to work on the opening of The Cosmopolitan Hotel in Las Vegas was a blessing with an eight-figure price tag. The highlight of the opening was a concert that featured Jay-Z, Beyoncé, John Mayer, and Kanye West. *People* magazine called it the concert of the year.

We did get through it, with priceless lessons, every day, that I never thought I needed, and I'm extremely grateful for them.

The worst mistake, and this was a big one for me, was that I hired the wrong people. Smart-talking consultants gave me bad advice, and I ran with it. That was on me, and me alone. Because of what happened in 2008, I'm a better businessman today. I'm very disciplined. To sum it up, I learned:

1. The true value of a dollar.
2. Never, ever overextend emotionally or financially.
3. Outsourcing to a competent contractor can save you time, money, and aggravation.
4. Take time to investigate new hires and consultants.
5. Don't dismiss what you don't want to hear. (More about this below.)

●

## What Went Wrong?

Clients complain when something goes wrong, whether it was something you could foresee or not. How do you listen to that customer? Even someone who is unpleasant and complaining can give you useful feedback. Some people complain politely and respectfully, some are visibly upset, and some are rude bordering on abusive and don't bother to manage their anger. I've witnessed them all. And I've learned the hard way not to dismiss something I don't like hearing merely because of how, why, or who expressed it.

Even if a customer is angry, can you step back and analyze what they're saying? Remove your emotional response from the equation and put yourself in your customer's shoes. Sometimes it's necessary to mentally remove your own shoes before putting yourself into your customer's shoes and accept unwelcome information from them, especially if you think that they're wrong, or the problem was of their own making.

Focus on the facts, not *your* feelings. Don't get defensive. It's not just *how* a customer complains; *it's what they are complaining about*. Do they have a valid point? Was there a mistake made that you can look at and improve in the future?

You might recall in chapter 5, the story of how we ordered beautiful invitations for a wedding, but the ink on the envelopes rubbed off. When the client called me to report the problem, the bride was not very pleasant, and rightfully so. We weren't meeting her expectations about the level of service she was paying for. However, she graciously accepted my apology and my solution to the situation, which then set the protocol for how we've handled all invitations going forward. We took what we learned, recovered, and improved our procedures so it would not happen again.

But then sometimes there's a client who isn't satisfied with a practical solution to a mistake. Once, we had another invitation issue. The invitation was one-sixteenth of an inch too big and it was difficult, although not impossible, to slip it in and out of the envelope. We were able to trim the invitations so the alterations were undetectable, but that wasn't good enough for the client. He demanded that we reprint all of the invitations rather than fix the existing ones. In this case, I prevailed. My responsibility was to correct the mistake; it wasn't necessary to lie down and let the client (metaphorically) walk all over me.

There are going to be failed client relationships. There are going to be toxic client relationships. I've fired my share of clients, but there are also difficult ones I've chosen to maintain. To paraphrase country singer Kenny Rogers, you have to know when to hold your cards, and sometimes you fold your cards and leave the table. One thing I have learned is that there will always be another job. My team is my long-term financial and personal investment and not easily replaced. A client who tortures them or makes them miserable is not, in my book, worth keeping.

People have their own way of gauging relationships. Some use a calculator and others an abacus about which relationships are worth trouble and stress. Whatever method you use, trust the answer.

We have a longtime client who lives on another coast who was going through a terribly difficult time personally, and she took it out on everyone. After I had submitted our design for a party, I asked if she wanted to meet in person to go through it with me. She didn't want me to fly to LA; she wanted to run it by some other people first. A week later, she called and complained about the design and then gave me a long list of criticisms. I pointed out that we'd worked together for ten years and had created enormously successful, magical events together. I had never let her down before, and yet she was allowing other people to jump in and rip apart our proposal before I had the opportunity to present it to her. In the end, we did work together, and I produced a stunningly beautiful party for her, using my original concept. I'm likely to continue to work with her, for a while. But she's already sent up a strong red flag of distrust that I will pay attention to. Should the relationship deteriorate in other ways that indicate her lack of respect for our work, I may decide to walk away. That's okay; I don't have to win every time.

•

## It's Not Always About You

"*Why me?*" isn't the right question when things go wrong. "Why me?" lets you indulge in self-pity and hand-wringing, and avoid looking critically and dispassionately at the situation. It wastes precious time. Those minutes, hours, and days can never be recovered. There's no future in the past; you need to keep moving ahead. There are other questions you could be asking that will help you understand what went wrong and give you the missing information you need to rebuild or start fresh. Don't ignore or completely repress your feelings. When you're angry or upset, you should feel those feelings and go over all the things that aren't working or going your way. This is your grieving time to mourn those losses, but then get a grip and leave those feelings behind. Rumination is a leader's undoing. Clear your mind to make room for your next chapter. It's what I did in the wake of COVID-19 before starting Thrive Hospitality.

At Colin Cowie Lifestyle, my team and I hold postmortems after every event. We applaud our successes, of course, but I'm more interested in the things that *didn't* go well. The first question I ask after we discuss a mistake is, "What really happened here?"

Mistakes cause confusion. It often takes time and discernment to break down what went wrong and how it could have happened. In addition, I want to know:

Can we identify who or what was responsible?

What can we learn from this mistake?

How does this mistake apply to anything else we're doing in my business?

What can I do proactively to prevent anything like this from happening again?

If your mistake affected a client or customer, sometimes acknowledging a mistake can be enough to satisfy them. Sometimes it isn't, and if it isn't, you need to take action ASAP to rectify the situation. To do that, you need to know what your client wants. Ask them. "What can I do to regain your trust and confidence? What is going to make you comfortable going forward? What can I do to demonstrate that we are willing to make things right again?"

Once you have that information, it's time to act on it, and recover. If you are willing to learn, each failure and each mistake is another step to success.

Sometimes there is no recovery. I was in talks with two television production companies about a doing a show. I chose one, but as negotiations progressed, I began to lose confidence in the producers. A third company came to me with a dream offer. I extricated myself from the negotiation, signed with the third company, and *boom*! Along came COVID-19 and no one was producing anything. I went from three possible deals to zero. The only thing to do was to refocus. Was I disappointed that these deals fell through? Of course I was.

However, the COVID-19 silver lining for me was becoming focused in a new way, and being able to devote my time to my new venture and plan for the future of Colin Cowie Lifestyle. There's still the possibility of a new television production and it will be better for the time I've given myself and my business's development.

Whether a fail was 100 percent your responsibility, the result of things beyond your control, or a combination of the two, you live with your decisions, your mistakes, and yourself in the end. Take all the lessons to heart and, regardless of what's happened, don't beat yourself up. Forgive yourself; forgive others; forgive the economy; forgive the weather. To be human is to make mistakes. As I've gotten older and wiser, I spend less time blaming myself and more time figuring out how to do things better next time. It's like building muscle: you have to break it down in order to get stronger.

If you're in business, you're going to take risks, and if you take risks, you're going to make mistakes. If you don't take risks, you're *still* going to make mistakes. So why not take the risk? The rewards are so much greater and so are the opportunities to learn and grow.

KEEP IN MIND:

- Prepare for the unthinkable. Failure is an inevitability and integral to success; if you're going to stay in business, you must train yourself to find the light in the dark.
- Making assumptions without doing the necessary homework and research means leaving things to chance.
- The easiest failures to recover from are the ones that are your team's fault or yours.
- "Why me?" isn't the question to ask when something goes wrong. The right question is: *"What can I do to prevent this from ever happening again?"*


NOW ASK YOURSELF:

- What procedures and protocols do I have in place to avoid mistakes?
- Am I prepared to make things right for my customers when something goes wrong?
- Am I willing to walk away from a difficult client for the sake of my team?

# t e n

*You Win the Race*

*by Looking Ahead!*

**Y**ou, today: You have your morning routine on autopilot. You've honed your service protocols to a razor's edge. You know your team has internalized your standards and practices, and you trust them to bring their own excellent instincts and emotional intelligence to any service situation. Your business routinely gets five-star reviews. Do you get to rest on your laurels? Sorry, but no. Never. Tomorrow is another day.

When it comes to customer service, you can't sit back and wait for things to happen. You constantly look ahead and for opportunity because things change. Nothing stays the same. Change doesn't mean things change for the better and things don't change for the worse. It's always different depending on what you want and what you are doing. What might mean good news to you could mean disaster for someone else. Technologies change, and our customers' expectations change. Sometimes there's a black swan event, and evolution becomes revolution. That's never been truer. We evaluate and reevaluate our procedures and business models constantly, and we're continually looking for opportunities to do things better. Are you doing the same?

During the first year of the pandemic, many commercial airlines across the world ceased operations or filed for bankruptcy. Southwest Airlines, however, saw opportunity, and began buying up shorter routes between cities, ones that the larger airlines were giving up. Over one hundred thousand restaurants nationwide closed. Those that survived or reopened were forced to rethink their customers' needs and wants. Some offered a subscription home delivery service, providing a fine dining experience in the comfort of home. Some catered to vegetarians or vegans; others focused on family-friendly meals. Uber and Lyft shifted to delivering other things besides passengers. More than 145,000 retail stores closed their doors; others shifted to a new way of selling, contracting with successful online sales companies during the pandemic, and afterward expanding their business in ways they had never considered before.

The silver lining of any bad situation is that it tests our resilience. Maybe it's just that Mother Nature got tired of seeing us too satisfied with ourselves. Let's face it: COVID-19 gave the world a giant international "force quit." It forced us to reboot and change how we think about ourselves, our lives, and our relationships—the where, how, what we do, and with whom we do it. It taught us to make choices and decisions in a way that would have been unimaginable BC (Before COVID). The result is an awakened world, more appreciative of who and what we have closest to us.

We've been through a forest fire, and the devastation leaves room for new growth. As the saying goes, nature abhors a vacuum, and as businesses close, the space they leave behind is often a new opportunity for someone else. Richard Baker, CEO of Hudson's Bay Company, whose portfolio includes luxury and premium department stores to off-price fashion shopping destinations, said in an interview there has been an exodus from traditional office spaces as people have transitioned to working from home. A survey by S&P Global Market Intelligence found that 64 percent of decisionmakers said they are making permanent changes that will allow a significant portion of their employees to work remotely. Companies renegotiated their office leases to downsize to accommodate this new reality; one-third of those surveyed by S&P Global have reduced their office space. Coworking spaces like We-Work offered flexible, comfortable, but not luxurious, workspaces for remote work. There's an opportunity to create a new product for an emerging market: What about a flexible workspace for the CEO or COO who doesn't always want to work from home and expects the amenities and services they're used to in an executive suite?

In New York City, a friend went to South Street Seaport. On Pier 17, where they once held concerts, once the pandemic began they created The Greens, fourteen-by-fourteen-foot squares of green space with cabana-style lounge chairs, a sun umbrella, built-in cooler, and a USB charging port. Each green space could accommodate up to eight guests, with on-site food and beverage service created by celebrity chef Jean Georges Vongerichten. Reservations for space were in ninety-minute increments, and the reservation fee was donated to The Bowery Mission, a charity that feeds New Yorkers in need.

While living in the moment, we also have to look ahead. All crises pass. How we do business may change, but the consumer always decides who they want to do business with. The question for us becomes: How do we best move forward in our brave new world order? Psychiatrist Elisabeth Kübler-Ross taught us that there are five stages of grief: denial, anger, bargaining, depression, and acceptance. Different people go through the stages at their own pace. There has to be another stage after acceptance, however, and that's reentry and moving forward. What does that look like?

People went back to their offices again though not in the same way—not for the same five-day/nine-to-five schedules, nor in the same numbers. Though nothing can replace meeting with people face-to-face, Zoom and other group meeting apps have taken the place of many in-person meetings and classes. Where many companies resisted having a dispersed team, it became the norm. It was no longer about working from home; it became about working from anywhere.

We started buying clothes other than sweatpants. Clothing and shoe shopping had already been moving online. Brick and mortar will never go away, but it was forced to change. Retailers realized they didn't need 150,000 square feet of store space. A concept store with less square footage, less inventory, fewer staff, and far less overhead could satisfy demand. Having one or two of every size allowed the buyer to see, handle, and try on a piece of clothing, order it, and then have it shipped directly to them. While business spaces were less crowded for a while, there was still fierce and exciting competition. In 2019, I traveled thousands of miles all over the world giving talks and seminars. In 2020, I couldn't keep up with the requests for Zoom calls and webinars.

People who had stayed at home for more than a year got the itch to travel again, Some people stayed close to home, and if they traveled, started studying Google maps for road trips.

Camping and hiking became the family vacation for thousands of people new to the outdoors.

Like the airlines, hotels and other hospitality or short-term vacation venues that were impacted by the virus became more flexible about cancellation fees, if they charged them at all.

During the pandemic, I had several speaking engagements a week about what was happening in the events and hospitality industry. The questions I was asked every time were, "*When* is our business coming back?" "*Is* it going to come back?" The reality is that nothing ever comes back. Instead, we evolve and move forward. Water always seeks and finds its new level. We focus on the future because we cannot change the past. We can learn from it, but we can't change it.

There will always be disrupters that force us to change. It may be a new competitor, or it could be a global event. Carvana, the internet car buying and selling venture, is a disrupter. COVID-19 is a disrupter and may have set off one of the biggest paradigm shifts in how we live and work. We've become more conscious and diligent about health and sanitary protocols, and I don't see that changing. What else doesn't change? The elements of the gold standard of the true customer service experience: personalization, attention to detail, elegance/efficiency, teamwork, communication, standards, and consistency.

My team and I pivoted to focus more on our work in long-term hospitality projects, instead of limiting ourselves to event planning; we're taking the opportunity to build a more sustainable revenue source. That said, we haven't closed our events business down. Our team prepared for the time people start gathering again and started booking future events one to two years ahead.

Thrive Hospitality started working on several resort consulting projects, which became a whole new ball game for us.

We spent time defining and refining the catalog of services we could offer. Once we put everything under one umbrella, we found we could offer our customers a suite of services that would have required that they hire three or four other companies for the same benefits. Our challenge was how to make the very necessary layer of COVID-19 safety protocols as sexy and glamorous as the resort or venue they were needed for. Our goal remains for the guests to enjoy their stay with the confidence that they're safe and being taken care of on every level.

During the pandemic, when guests checked in, we offered them washable linen gloves in a choice of sizes and colors. Instead of staff and servers wearing surgical masks, we designed neutral or skin-toned masks to match the wearers' skin, or embellished them with whimsical mustaches or lipsticked mouths, or with a logo. If there was an event at the resort, we could provide masks for the guests—silver or gold for the women and black or navy blue to match tuxedos for the men. We considered offering guests a choice of three colored bracelets when they checked in at an event, signaling guests' comfort level with social contact. One color means "Happy to see you, but please respect social distance guidelines." Another color says, "Closer than six feet is fine, but no touching and I prefer you keep your mask on." The third color signals "Bring on the careful hugs!"

Opportunity is always everywhere. Proactive customer service means caring about how your client or customer feels, and they want to feel safe. What does safe look like? As I wrote this, hand sanitizer and temperature checks were required to enter many places. As rapid tests and vaccinations are more widely available, it could become standard operating procedure to have guests present a vaccination certificate or be tested at the door of an event before they're permitted to enter.

From the outset of the pandemic, I thought it could mean the return of literal white glove service. Buffets as we used to know them have changed but that paved the way for fabulously curated and styled individual food stations staffed by servers behind a plexiglass screen. A screen decorated to match the theme of the event displays the name of the dish, and lists the ingredients so guests with food allergies or sensitivities will be better able to decide if it is safe for them to eat.

How have we safely begun to greet each other? Adopt the bow as they do in East Asian countries? The Thai *wai*? Do we now nod or touch our heart? These things may differ depending on your culture. Does our spoken greeting change? Do we say, "Be well" instead of "goodbye"? I don't have the answers to these questions, yet my team and I are thinking about them as they apply to our business and what we can do to keep it fresh and safe. Are you?

Your customer may be happy today, but what about tomorrow? Next month? Next year? What your customer wants and needs, and your competition, are constantly evolving and changing. Unless you do the same, you'll be left behind. The commercial climate is changing so fast that we are in a constant state of always sharpening the pencil and being more competitive. I've found that when you make one change, there's usually a domino effect, and other changes follow. We're looking not just at what we offer our customer, but how—and we're always looking for an opportunity to do it better, more efficiently, and at less cost to us and our client.

We're constantly gathering information from the marketplace about what our customer wants. We're constantly getting feedback from our customers and responding to it—not in the moment, but as we look ahead. We want to know who our new customer is and exactly what they're looking for.

Customer loyalty means everything to us. We look for ways to continually engage and strengthen our emotional connection with our customers.

That means getting very, very granular. I've found that too often people think they know what their customer wants, but they don't know. At a hotel, a manager told me check-in took five minutes. We timed it, and it took fifteen. They knew that their clientele was thirty to fifty-five, but age didn't really give them the information they needed to make an emotional connection. We helped them discover that most of their clients were women with disposable income who were looking for a short break from work and family as well as opportunities for both exercise and relaxation. Working with them, we helped them create vacation packages that spoke directly to their "new" market.

Many of their previous bookings, which they had begun to take for granted, came through travel agents or travel concierges. We showed them how they could reach the potential consumers who researched on the internet and could book directly through their website. Now, how could they reach them more immediately? Through Facebook and Instagram primarily. (Snapchat is for thirteen- to twenty-nine-year-olds, not their clients. Then came TikTok, which also had much younger users. That also would have been a distraction for them.)

Races are lost when a swimmer looks to the left or right to see what the competition is doing. Looking ahead keeps you ahead. Winners keep their focus on their performance and what's in front of them, not what the other guy is doing. Trust yourself and stay focused on your vision and mission; that's how you win the race. This doesn't mean that you may not need to recalculate your path if things change. I've always believed that we need to be agile. The key to being agile is to be able to leave your ego at the door and let your consumer tell you what they're willing to do. At the end of the day, it doesn't matter what *you* want, or what you want to sell. They'll let you know if they're buying what you're selling.

If there's one mistake that I've been guilty of, it's thinking, "Oh, maybe we should be doing this; maybe we should be doing that." I've been incredibly fortunate to have been the recipient of many, many tempting offers. It's a massage for one's ego, but, worse, it's also a dangerous distraction. I've found the key is having the discipline to understand what works and what doesn't work for you.

I make the clear distinction between enhancing and extending your brand versus taking on projects that drain time, energy, and resources, and in the end dilute your brand. For example, at one time I had a deal with HSN and was designing a line of china for Lenox. Those were successful extensions of the Colin Cowie Lifestyle brand. The development of a line of products with somebody else, the offer to be a spokesperson for someone else's company, the development of a cultural center in the Middle East—all those flattering things took time and energy away from my core business, the company's forward movement, and my goal of being the premier go-to for luxury hospitality and entertainment.

Today, I like to think I'm more focused and more discriminating. While I am still offered tempting opportunities, today I am more likely to say *no* than *yes*. To get there, I ask myself these questions: Does the opportunity move us closer to where we want to be? Does it get us there faster? Offer us more income?

It's like building a house. You have your blueprints and a budget. As you go along, you're looking at design sites and you think that a bigger kitchen or a pool in your backyard might be nice. At some point, it's up to you to decide what elements make sense for your needs, your budget, and the resale value of the house. An architect once told me that, practically speaking, the average person only uses six hundred square feet of their living space, bedroom, bath, and kitchen—everything else is extra, like icing on the cake. But who likes a cake without icing? Not me!

If we were brought on to design the elements of hospitality at a resort, for example, and then were asked to manage the property, we might want to say *yes* to both proposals. However, we'd have to ask ourselves if adding management to our portfolio would distract us from what we were hired to do, and question if it would align with our core competencies. Being an operator means taking on staffing responsibilities, taking on more team members for our organization, and requires more resources. While we could do it in theory, what price would *we* have to pay? Usually the expense is time, the steep learning curve, and money that would have to be spent, which is often greater than the profit. If the project is a one-off, is it worth the time and effort? If we're going to add management to our services, can we scale it so it will be profitable in the long run? "Time is money" is not just a saying.

We also look at the 80-20 rule: 20 percent of your business delivers 80 percent of your profits. Will this project be within that 20 percent? If the answer is *yes*, then we might consider taking it on, though not until we've done our due diligence and a careful evaluation. We make a conscious decision about whether a project is worth it or not. If we see it as a viable option, can we add these skills to our portfolio in an incremental way? Could consulting lead to taking a small piece of the operations, which could over time be scaled to encompass more of the project?

Recently, there were people in the event space who were completely focused on doing virtual parties and virtual fundraisers. I didn't know that business, and I had no desire to be in it. For others, it may have been a useful and profitable add-on. For me, it seemed a distraction.

Over the years, I've received high fees for speaking. During the pandemic, I was asked to participate in conferences and webinars or to be a spokesperson, but with no real compensation. "We can't afford to pay you now," I was told. "But we can give you *exposure* to *these* many eyeballs." My celebrity and reputation are my IP, my professional capital. Why use it if there's not a return on my investment of time? If, however, the audience they are asking me to speak to is in the hospitality business, or if they are people I want to connect with? Then, yes, that works for me.

I want to be looking to the future while keeping an eye on the past. I don't ever want to become complacent, as that lowers the standard of service we give our clients. If forward progress is a series of peaks and valleys, I strive to make the last valley higher than the valley behind it. I may not succeed every time, but that's my goal. And I'm sure it can be yours too.

# Acknowledgments

I have wanted to write this book for a very long time. I am so grateful that my literary agent, Margret McBride, who has represented me on each of my eleven books, was as excited and passionate about this project as I was. And thank you to her associate, Faye Atchison.

Writing a book takes a tremendous amount of effort and time. I am so grateful to Sydny Miner. Working with her has been a pleasure from the first word in the book to the last chapter. Thank you for your insight, passion, and guidance.

Thanks to my business partner, Stephan Baroni—for your contribution, the debates, and discussions that led to this manuscript.

Sara Kendrick, my brilliant editor at HarperCollins Leadership: thank you for believing in this project and supporting it with your guidance and expert eye. Sicily Axton, senior marketing manager, and Jeff James, former HarperCollins Leadership publisher, thanks for helping fight for my book.

I would be remiss if I did not acknowledge the team of talented and committed people I get to work with on a daily basis and who share my passion for creating the gold standard of customer service. Thank you all!

# Index

# About the Author

R espected around the world as an authority on living effortlessly with style, **Colin Cowie** has been at the forefront of event and wedding planning for the past thirty years. With his company Colin Cowie Lifestyle, he has created trends and raised the bar for the ultimate guest experience, planning spectacular parties for a who's who of royalty, celebrities, and business luminaries. Colin has created the most talked-about events in the world, including the multimillion-dollar openings of the Cosmopolitan Hotel in Las Vegas and Palm Island in Atlantis, Dubai, as well as Oprah Winfrey's Legends Ball.

Colin is the author of ten previous books and has appeared regularly on *CBS This Morning*, *Today*, HSN, and CNN. His work has been featured in the *New York Times*, the *Wall Street Journal*, *Time Magazine*, *O, The Oprah Magazine*, *People*,

*InStyle*, *Town & Country*, and *House Beautiful*, and on television shows including *The Oprah Winfrey Show*, *Ellen*, and *Access Hollywood*. In 2020, he launched Thrive Hospitality, which offers consulting services to top-tier hotels and hospitality venues. He sits on the board of several philanthropic organizations focusing on arts, education, healthcare, and mentorship programs in South Africa.